MW00887346

Flourish

A 40-DAY BIBLE STUDY FOR WOMEN

BY:

Nicole Nichols

A 40-DAY BIBLE STUDY FOR WOMEN

Written By Nicole Nichols

Copyright ©2023, Nicole Nichols, Jermaine Nichols; FLOURISH

ISBN: 9798370424687

All rights reserved.

This book or parts thereof may not be reproduced in any form, stored in a retrieval system, or transmitted in any form by any means—electronic, mechanical, photocopy, recording, or otherwise—without prior written permission of the publisher, except as provided by United States of America copyright law.

Unless otherwise noted, all Scripture quotations are taken from the New King James Version. Copyright ©1982 by Thomas Nelson. Used by permission. All rights reserved.

Published by: Awaken Media

Printed in the United States of America

Table of Contents

Flourish

1. verb - To grow or develop in a healthy or vigorous way, especially as the result of a particularly favorable environment.

2. noun- a bold or extravagant gesture or action, made especially to attract the attention of others. "with a flourish, she ushered them inside."

3. an instance of suddenly performing or developing in an impressively successful way.

Dedication

To my amazing husband. Thank you for your encouragement, your love and for always believing in me. You have always encouraged me and allowed me to fly. Who would have thought that two kids who didn't come from a lot, would by chance meet miles from home on their very first day of college, get married and share an amazing life together?! I would not be who I am without you. I love you, "We are truly never bored".

To my son Elijah. You are my miracle. I am so blessed that God chose me to be your mother. I could not be more proud of you. One day, when I grow up, I hope to be as passionate and caring as you.

To my mother, Stacey Dunlap, your strength has always been my guiding example. I love you and thank you for loving me. To all my aunts and uncles, you all stood in the gap and made sure I had everything that I needed. As a young child, you took me to church and introduced me to God. Thank you for all your love and support.

To my Greater Works Center Family. I am honored to have so many friends who happen to call me "First Lady". This is the day the Lord has made and I am so thankful to share it with you all.

Introduction

You intended to harm me, but God intended it all for good. He
brought me to this position so I could save the lives of many .
- Genesis 50:20

That night my mother didn't know I was peeping around the
corner in our small house. I heard her arguing with a man whose
voice wasn't familiar to me. It was my father. I was the subject of
their argument. She was asking him for desperately needed
financial support. She asked him a question that changed my life
forever.

"How much is she worth to you?!!" my mother asked hoping
he would finally rise to his responsibilities.

Instead he reached into his pocket, retrieved a nickel and tossed
it on the coffee table. With that, he left my mother broken hearted
and me simply broken.

I have spent my life picking up the shattered pieces of the mess my
father made of my life that day. But as God has healed me from my
brokenness he has also given me a message to share. And as I have
listened to other women and read the word of God I am convinced that
God always plants a message in the middle of the mess. Embracing the
message and the mess is actually the key to flourishing.

Women were designed to flourish. I say that not as an inspiring
compliment but as a statement of fact. Women, unlike God's dust-made
creatures (men), were created in a paradise called Eden. We are as much
products of the Garden of Eden as was the Tree of Life that grew at
its center. The name Eden is defined as "God's pleasure" which means
we are intended to bring God joy by constantly being in his presence.
This book is a guide for returning to the garden of his presence so that we
may once again Flourish.

To flourish means to grow healthily and vibrantly. But don't picture a manicured and well organized bed of flowers. Think rather of a jungle, both lush and wild. With each step, there is something new to discover. There is balance, but not in the way most would expect.

Flourishing isn't about calm perfection. I don't know any woman's life that has been that easy. Your experience, like mine, is not a row lilies in a level field. When we flourish it's more like ivy. We have to grow over stones and across fences. No matter what is put in its path, ivy will find a way. Whether by going over, around, or through, eventually, the ivy will change its environment to such a degree that those looking from the outside can't see the obstacles it overcame.

Fair warning: this book isn't for the faint-hearted. If you are looking for someone to tell you haven't made any mistakes and this mean ole world is out to get you, you have selected the wrong book. This study is for those ready for victory, not for those who have decided to remain victims. You have chosen this book because you are ready to be victorious!

The journey you are about to embark upon may be painful, but it is purposed. Comfort zones will be crushed. Insecurities will be exposed and excuses ignored. This won't be an *Eat, Pray, Love,* feel-good girls' journey to feed your ego. You will discover that in your past you have thought, felt and acted incorrectly. Flourishing is about surrendering to God's will and all of the unexpected challenges that come with it. Together we will rummage through your past, hold your actions accountable, and shine light on your suffering as we discover your destiny.

Grab a pen and a journal because it's about to get real!

Feel

The rumors were true. As she peered through the window of the Pharisee's home, she could see him about to dine. She didn't understand what Jesus was doing with them?! But that didn't matter now. The one she had been waiting for was here.

She felt something in her spirit urging her forward. So many emotions were washing over her all at once: love, fear, courage, and an unfamiliar peace. She anxiously walked into the house full of "godly men." The only women present were servants. That was perfect because serving was what she desired to do. No one noticed as she positioned herself behind the "master."

Despite her best efforts to control her feelings, she could not contain herself. Her vision was blurred by her tears. They poured out from the faucet of her soul. She fell to her knees in overwhelming appreciation of being in His presence. Her tears cascaded over His feet as an offering of gratefulness. Unlike most men, He didn't react to her existence with disgust. He received her offering with grace.

Lacking a towel to dry his tear covered feet she decided to use what the Spirit made available to her - her hair. A woman's hair was a symbol of her value. Despite her past, she knew in her heart that her value amounted to more than a part of her body, she uncovered her crown of brown locks and carefully wiped the dust and grime from his feet.

Much to the displeasure of those in the righteous audience, she opened a small alabaster box of oil. The fragrance immediately flooded the room. This type of precious oil was meant for only one of two occasions, a wedding or a funeral. Today would be both. As she anointed the feet of her savior, she was forever committed to Him and, at the same time, she buried the shame of her past.

- Luke 7:36-50

The Light of the Soul

Then she knelt behind him at his feet, weeping. Her tears fell on his feet, and she wiped them off with her hair. Then she kept kissing his feet and putting perfume on them.
- Luke 7:38

One of the saddest things we do as women is think that our emotions are a sign of weakness. If a woman feels too much, she is considered dramatic and can't be taken seriously. If she is not emotional enough, she is cold and lacks femininity. But the Bible shows us that a woman who walks with God can count on her feelings to lead her to His will and her destiny.

In the story of the woman who wiped Jesus's feet with her hair, we discover a woman who allowed her emotions to spill over. Her emotions led her to do something that didn't make sense but was filled with purpose. Feelings is our soul's response to the condition of our hearts.

Think of emotions as the check engine lights of the soul. When I purchased my first car, I was always afraid that the warning lights meant my car was broken. But as I have grown, I have learned that the check engine light is actually an indication of something that needs attention. The car is not yet broken. Those lights are put there by the manufacturer to protect the driver from breaking down. Usually, the light comes on *before* things are beyond repair. It is when we ignore the light that we find ourselves stuck in a difficult situation.

Overwhelming emotions are a signal that something needs attention.

But that doesn't always mean that something bad is happening. Sometimes our overwhelming feelings are an indication that God is presenting us with an opportunity. God lets us feel things in our spirit before we see them in the natural. The world calls this intuition. The Bible calls it spiritual discernment.

It's okay to *feel*. Even Jesus wept (John 11:35) while overcome with emotion as he learned of the death of his friend Lazarus. But if Jesus had not responded to this emotional opportunity by calling on his heavenly father, Larazus would not have risen from the tomb. It is often in the overflow of emotion that we find healing, clarity and power.

Even what we call negative emotions have their place. Jealousy maybe your soul's way of telling you that you deserve better than you have settled for. Anger could be your signal to fight for what you believe in. Sadness maybe a way of honoring a loss. The key is to submit all these feelings to God so that he can guide you towards your purpose.

Reflection:
1. **What were you taught a woman's emotions meant?**

2. **How often do you find yourself suppressing your emotions? What do you fear will happen if you express them?**

3. **If emotions are a warning light for the soul. What are your current emotions warning you about ?**

The Breaker and the Broken

When the Pharisee who had invited him saw this, he said to himself, "If this man were a prophet, he would know what kind of woman is touching him. She is a sinner!"
- Luke 7:39

Jesus, like many of us, was often tested. This is what women frequently do to one another. In today's language, it's called "throwing shade." Shade is when people manipulate social situations in an effort to expose someone as inadequate. On the occasion in Luke 7, the person who tried to test Jesus was a legal scholar called a Pharisee.

The Pharisee's goal was to prove that Christ was a false prophet. How did this Pharisee seek to prove the phoniness of Jesus? By being phony himself. Sound familiar? The Pharisee invited Jesus to dinner so that he and his self righteous friends could stand in judgment. Jesus knew full well what they were up to. Even though he knew their motives, Jesus still accepted the invitation of those he knew sought to expose him.

Like Jesus, a woman who wants to flourish doesn't run from spaces that are occupied by people who don't like her.

In my life, I have found that the people who reject you are eventually the ones God will use to elevate you. As it says in Acts 2:34-35, God will sit you at his right hand, humble your enemies and make them footstools beneath your feet. If God can turn the hearts of your enemies, then who can resist you?

Notice that Christ didn't rebuke those who attempted to embarrass him. Jesus came to save the broken *and* those who do the breaking. Yes, even the petty, shady, and pretentious. He came for those who hide their own insecurities by demeaning others. The real question is, "Which one are you?" Are you attempting to expose someone because they make you feel inadequate or do you find that it feels as if there is always someone or something pushing you to your breaking point. Too often the pain of being broken leads us to become a breaker of things and people. Regardless, whether you are broken or doing the breaking it is sign that you are allowing your feelings to rob you of the joy God desires for your soul.

Reflection:
1. **Do you find yourself unintentionally attacking others or do you feel as if you are always being picked on? Are you the broken or are you the one doing the breaking?**

2. **To flourish, you must let God guide and protect you in all situations. Which "good emotions" do you think align you with the will of God? How can you align your negative emotions to help you find purpose?**

3. **Before you move onto day 3, take a moment in prayer and repent for the times you have been the one breaking those around you. Ask the Holy Spirit to give you discernment and to teach you how to forgive yourself and reconnect with those you have hurt.**

DAY 3

Let Peace Protect You

Then Jesus answered his thoughts. "Simon," he said to the Pharisee, "I have something to say to you."
- Luke 7:40

Have you seen those posts on social media by women who declare that they are no longer going to associate with people who disagree with them? Have you ever made or shared one of those posts?

There is no shame in it. Those post are about proving to the world that you are in control of your life. It is a declaration that you can't and won't be fooled into a toxic friendship again. As self empowering as this may sound the reality is that type of thinking means we are allowing a bad experience to make our world smaller. If you refuse to go to a place because someone there doesn't like the way God has told you to live your life, then the people you are avoiding are actually in control. You have given them the power to put up emotional, spiritual and even physical road blocks in your life by simply keeping you from a space you wish to occupy. Jesus refused to reduce his existence because of the opinions of others. So what?! If someone didn't like him. In fact, Jesus often sought out places where he wasn't welcome. He never hid the way he felt about God, not even for those that hated him.

Too often, we say that we are "protecting our peace." Protecting our peace isn't necessary because peace *is* our protection... it doesn't need protecting.

Your peace is not an umbrella to protect you. Your peace is the sword that frees you.

Your peace cuts through the snide comments, demeaning looks, and intimidating body language of those who seek to transfer their insecurities onto you. Peace is actually a manifestation of the Holy Spirit. That is why Jesus called the Holy Spirit "the comforter". The Holy Spirit hardly needs to be protected.

And please stop being offended by the idea of people talking about you behind your back. Everyone who reached greatness in scripture was the subject of gossip. Especially the women. Just ask the woman at the well, Ruth or Mary the mother of Jesus. They were all gossiped about relentlessly. In fact if people aren't talking about you then something is very wrong.

God declares that He gives us peace that is greater than any understanding. Your peace should be so powerful that it doesn't make sense. Peace does not make you run and hide. Peace gives you the power to kick open the door to any room with the declaration that "I won't surrender my joy because you have made the decision to be unhappy!"

Christ didn't have to protect his peace because his peace was his protection. He never withheld his feelings because his feelings were a part of the abundant life he came to give to others. You have a gift that God wants you to give. Allow your peace to carve out a path to the ones you have come to help.

Reflection:

1. What situation(s) you were led to confront but chose not to in the name of "protecting your peace"?

2. What do you think would have happened if you had confronted your fears?

3. What activity or place provides the most peace for you? Why do you think God chooses to meet you there?

4. Declare today: I will no longer surrender my joy in the name of protecting my peace. Peace is my sword.

Vulnerable and Victorious

Then he turned to the woman and said to Simon, "Look at this woman kneeling here. When I entered your home, you didn't offer me water to wash the dust from my feet, but she has washed them with her tears and wiped them with her hair.
- Luke 7:44-47

In Luke chapter 7 the writer tells us to literally "look" at this woman. "*Behold*" her, the scripture instructs. She was a sinner. This meant that there was something about her that made it obvious that she was not a keeper of the law. Perhaps it was the way she dressed. Maybe the way she spoke indicated that she was from the "wrong side of the tracks."

As women, there is nothing we fear more than the obvious. The run in the stockings. The declined credit card. The nakedness of a ring finger after a divorce. These things send us running for cover faster than a teenager home alone in an 80's horror flick. No one can know the dirty little secret, that we aren't perfect.

I think the bible tells us to "behold" her because no one else really acknowledged her. She was simply "the sinner." She was of no value. To everyone else she was just something to be used.

What happens next changes everything. This rejected woman sees Jesus and does something amazing. She grabs her most expensive ointment and decides to being worshiping and praising God. Who does that?! Who worships and praises when they have been cast aside, labeled, and shamed?! A woman who is about to FLOURISH!

A flourishing woman never waits for a convenient time to worship God.

It is quite possible that being labeled a sinner had dashed this woman's self-esteem. Fortunately she didn't worship because *she* felt worthy. She worshiped because *Christ* is worthy. She didn't wait until she repaired *her* reputation. She moved forward because of *His* reputation. She didn't delay until she acquired a more respectable job. And she certainly was not waiting until she found a man before she offered her worship. Nor did she first shop for the right outfit.

The point I am trying to make is we must not let problems dictate our praise. Praise is not about what is but what *can* be. Praise happens when we align the words of our mouth with the unconditional joy in our hearts. Praise sets the scene for amazing possibilities. Praise creates an environment of encouragement for the receiver. In this moment, this woman allows her emotions to reflect her vulnerability. But her vulnerability also makes her powerful because it connects her to Christ. Not once during her breakdown does she say, "Woe is me!" Instead, her emotions are focused on the worthiness of her savior. She is victorious because her vulnerability drew her closer to Christ and made him, not her troubles, the focus of her praise.

Reflection:

1. What is your first reaction when confronted with a problem/challenge? Do you go into "fix it" mode? Or do you hope that if you ignore it, it will eventually go away?

2. In those moments when your heart is heavy or things are falling apart why do you think people resist giving God praise?

3. Do you find yourself panicking more than praising God? Look back over your past and try to understand what made you develop that perspective.

The Invisible Woman

Then she <u>knelt behind</u> him at his feet, weeping.
- Luke 7:38

In verse 38 (of Luke 7), the Bible is careful to mention *how* the woman approaches Jesus. Notice the position of this woman. She approaches Jesus from behind. This symbolizes her desire to serve. In her service to Christ, she did not demand attention. As women, we must push against the idea that we must be seen to be appreciated. Believing that having our name in lights or on an office door somehow makes us of more value is a self destructive heart posture. Praise should not be our expected reward for everything we do. The spiritual hole of needing to be recognized is one that can never be filled.

We live in a world that is desperate for attention. We thirst anxiously for "likes" and "follows". It's heartbreaking what some women will do when confronted with the lights of a camera. We spend hours taking "selfies" with the hope that the approval of others will help us feel better about ourselves. We search for just the right pose. We try to position our bodies, contort our faces, and purse our lips to achieve a look that says we have an exciting life. How amazing it would be if we could have back all the hours spent pretending to be living well and instead actually enjoyed living?

This is especially true of women in ministry. We should minister out of gratefulness for what God has done for us. However, who really gets the glory when a selfie is taken while feeding the homeless or mentoring a young girl? Those in need deserve the respect of privacy. Moreover, God deserves the praise for making that moment possible. Perhaps this is why Jesus often told those he healed to tell no one about their healing. Jesus wasn't concerned with others being impressed. He only cared to please his father.

This does not mean to allow yourself to be passed over for the things you do in the workplace or to be cheated out of what you have rightfully earned. Women who flourish are not doormats for anyone. However, there is a service that is due to God. We must not allow our egos to overshadow that. The Bible says that if we desire to be acknowledged for what we give to God, then attention will be our only reward. There is nothing more pitiful than watching a woman over-dramatize her offering of praise for the sake of those looking.

When we try to appear holy we miss the presence of God.

The woman in Luke 7 does her best to be invisible so that Jesus would be appreciated. She wanted people to experience the love of Jesus that she was feeling. She dared not rob her savior of His glory.

Reflection:

1. **Think about a time in your life when you felt ignored? How did you resolve those moments?**

2. **What kind of behavior have these feeling manifested in your life?**

3. **When someone compliments you do you feel embarrassed or encouraged? How can you give God glory despite these feelings?**

DAY 6

Why Cry?

**Then she knelt behind him at his feet, weeping.
Her tears fell on his feet,
- Luke 7:13**

A lot of people like this story in the Bible. It usually comes up when people want to talk about true worship. But what no one seems to ever ask is, "Why was she crying?" Some think it is because she is thankful, but we don't see anywhere that Christ did anything for her. Perhaps she heard a message he preached, but I think there may be other reasons for her tears.

Jewish custom required that when a guest came to your home to dine, someone, usually the host or a servant, washes the visitor's feet. No one offered to clean Jesus's feet. Keep in mind that dining was not done at an elevated table as we do in modern times. The table was positioned much lower, with the feet actually visible. The Pharisees didn't wash the feet of Jesus because they wanted Jesus to appear unclean. This lack of attention was meant to embarrass and reduce Jesus.

Like me, you may have at some point in your life experienced someone trying to embarrass you by drawing attention to what you didn't have. They invited you into their circle with the true intention of making a spectacle out of you. Perhaps they wanted it known that you were single by inviting you to a couples event. Or maybe they wanted to draw attention to your financial situation by inviting you to shop at a place they knew you couldn't afford. If you find yourself in this situation, don't back down! The way you will be victorious is by being your authentic self. Don't hide. Be honest about your situation but still participate. Let your light shine by enjoying yourself fully! Go on the trip with the biggest smile on your face! Celebrate what God has done in the life of others knowing he will do the same for you.

Authenticity overcomes embarrassment every time.

If you find yourself in a situation that was meant to shame you, do what Jesus did! Lean in!

Reflection:

1. **What shameful/embarrassing moment from your past has been tormenting you?**

2. **Do you trust the Lord enough to give it to him and receive victory over that shame?**

3. **If you were in this woman's situation, would you have washed Jesus' feet in the presence of the Pharisees? Why or Why not?**

.

Uncovered

Her tears fell on his feet, and she wiped them off with her hair.
- Luke 7:38

God had met the woman's need for something to wash Jesus's feet, but her worship was not complete. Something was needed to dry his feet before applying the oil. Perhaps after seeing the value of her tears, she realized that she was enough. What she would do next was the most scandalous action this known harlot would ever do in her life. Imagine the collective gasp as she removed her scarf and allowed her hair to cascade over her shoulders and on to Jesus's feet.

What she had done was more than just unusual. It would have been considered unholy for two reasons. As a woman who was considered a "sinner," the only virtue she had left was her hair. As an act of modesty, a Jewish woman was required to keep her hair covered until after she was wed to her husband. Even then, her hair was only revealed in private to her spouse. To remove her scarf meant that she was publicly and permanently committing herself to Jesus.

Although those watching this woman probably considered her foolish to give up her last remaining value, she was actually increasing her worth at that moment. In fact, she made the wise choice of forfeiting the false covering of religion for the spiritual protection of an authentic relationship with Christ.

Every woman has to make this choice. We may not make it in a dramatic fashion like this woman, but we must all decide for whom we will allow ourselves to be exposed. This woman hadn't taken a risk at all. She simply traded a limited covering for a holy one.

You can't flourish when you hide your true self to please people.

We can only grow and prosper under the light of the loving Spirit of God.

Reflection:

1. **What issue are you hiding because church folks wouldn't find it holy?**

2. **How do you think Jesus, who died for you sins, would react to seeing your sin? What would he say about the shame you feel regarding your past?**

3. **Imagine how it would feel to be able to reveal your true self?**

All In

Then she kept kissing his feet and putting perfume on them.
- Ephesians 6:10

It is heartbreaking how we allow our self-worth to rise and fall based on the opinions of people who don't know or care about us. It's so sad the way our day can be so easily ruined by a nasty look from a woman across the room. Why are our spirits so fragile? Perhaps it's because our hope is placed in things that don't reflect value back to us. In the Old Testament, one of the commandments given to the children of Israel was to worship no graven image. A "graven image" is something that does not have or give life. God desperately wants us to avoid giving ourselves to anything that cannot "give us life" in return. Thats what we should consider before we allow something to effect us emotionally. Ask yourself, "Is this person or situation giving me life?"

For this woman who risked everything to break into the house of a Pharisee, Jesus was worth investing everything of value. The oil she poured was worth more than several months salary. But she knew giving her whole self to Christ would bless her life more than any perfume. The beauty of the grace of Christ is that he will accept anything that you value. That includes things that others have rejected. Christ values it all. He takes the beautiful and broken things alike and turns them into a purpose-filled life.

When we flourish, we go "all in" on trusting Jesus to transform everything about our lives.

How are you honoring what Christ has done in your life? What offering have you given him to celebrate his blessings and favor? It's not about material things. Jesus wants you, only you. All the things the woman gave as she washed his feet were simply symbols of her giving her heart to the her savior. To some her tears, hair and perfume meant nothing. But Christ knew her heart. Don't judge what you have. If it is special to you, then it is precious to God.

If you sing, offer him your voice. Sing to those who need hope. If you cook, make a meal that helps someone feel nourished the same way Christ has nourished your soul. Perhaps you enjoy cleaning. Clean the home of someone who is ill so that they may feel the holy presence of God. Christ will accept it all as a loving tribute to the life he gave as a sacrifice for you.

Reflection:

1. **List a few "graven images" in your life. These are things, and maybe even people, that you put value in but don't add value to you.**

2. **If Christ appeared to you and told you "Your tears are precious to me." What would be your response?**

Love

She welcomed the loneliness. The other women from the village stopped inviting her to draw water years ago. They made it clear that they could not risk their reputation by being seen with her.

She decided it was best that she filled her bucket in the noon day sun when no one was around. Despite the heat and humidity she kept her head down and made her way to the outskirts of the village. She could avoid eye contact, but she could not un-hear the things righteous women whispered about her as she passed. It was ironic how the gossip of judgmental women cut deeper than the vulgar comments of Samaritan men.

As she neared the well of Jacob, she couldn't help but relate to the condition of the bucket she carried. It too was hollow, unfulfilled, and lacking purpose.

She had hoped to be able to draw her water without confrontation. Her heart sank when she saw the silhouette of a man sitting at the well. As she drew nearer, she saw by his robe that he was a Jew. This situation couldn't be worse. Samaritan men could be mean but Jewish men were especially cruel because they didn't miss an opportunity to remind Samaritans that they were God's chosen people.

Just as she decided to turn back, he called to her, "Give me something to drink."

She was more than a little startled. His request contained three acknowledgments that no man, Jew or Samaritan, had ever made of her. The first was that he spoke to her at all. A man of the "chosen" people interacting with a Gentile?! Second, he spoke respectfully. He did not call her unclean or wretched. Lastly, he made a request, not a command. He was asking for her assistance as if she had worth?! What was most unfamiliar about it all was the tone of his voice. He spoke with a kindness that she had never experienced.

As they talked, she tried to resist him. She thought this was some trick that would end badly. But there was no deception in this Israelite. He was honest. He was direct. He wouldn't let himself be discouraged by the wall she quickly tried to build. Instead, his words dismantled the barrier of anger, rejection, and sadness she had built through so many heartbreaks. He inquired about things she had spent a lifetime trying to conceal.

Then he did something truly startling. He invited her to know him. It was an offer of intimacy but not like the physical propositions she had received from men throughout her life. He told her she would never have to come "here" again. The "here" he spoke of was not the well. "Here" was the feeling of disgrace. "Here" was the feeling of emptiness. He told her that "knowing" him was all that she would ever need.

Her new found freedom was exciting. She felt so empowered that she had to tell everyone. Including those that rejected and shamed her. They had no more power over her. She had drawn from the true well. The well of unconditional love that flowed from Christ.

- John 4:4-42

DAY 9

Going Through

He had to go through Samaria on the way. The woman was surprised, for Jews refuse to have anything to do with Samaritans.
- John 4:4 and 9

There is one constant thought when I look back over my life. That is that "God must really love me." The reason I am so sure of this is that there were times when I didn't make myself easy to love. You may have a perfect record of obedience. Unfortunately I cannot boast of such excellence. God has gone out of his way to show me that his love for me is truly unconditional. During the winter of 2010, I thought my life was nearly perfect. I was excelling in a new career that only God could have made possible. My husband and I started a church that was beginning to grow. And I was also pregnant.

I was past my third month. So I thought it was safe to tell people that I was expecting. I was had all the signs of pregnancy I had experienced with the birth of our son, who was then six years old. "Thank God we hadn't waited too long to try to have another child," I thought. If we were fortunate, perhaps we would have a girl. That way everything in my life would continue to be ideal.

I remember being so excited about our OBGYN visit to hear the baby's heartbeat. On the way there I reflected on the same visit with my son and was prepared for tears of joy. Sadly that day would be the start of tears for many days to come. As the doctor moved the ultrasound wand across the cold gel on my belly, there was no sound. Her eyes apologized without saying a word.

The doctor comforted us and set a date for the D&C telling us it was a minor outpatient procedure. My heart was shattered, and I simply wanted to move past it all. After the surgery, my husband and I returned home for what we hoped would be much-needed spiritual, emotional, and physical rest.

That evening, just as I came out of the haze of the anesthesia, I found myself in excruciating abdominal pain. At first, we assumed it was the normal healing from the operation. However, the pain increased to the point of feeling as if I was being attacked from the inside. We returned to the hospital to be told that there must have been a complication from the surgery. The doctors said my left ovary had somehow become twisted. It would have to be removed. This news was doubly painful. Not only had I lost the child that was still alive in my heart, but now I was also being told that the chance of ever having a another child again was highly unlikely.

The "minor" procedure was now a serious operation that had occupied our lives from Thanksgiving until just a few days before Christmas. My perfect world was now enveloped in a dark cloud that blocked out any hope of happiness. During my recovery, people visited, encouraged, and prayed with me. I went through the motions and said all the holy things I thought a First Lady should say, but God and I were not on speaking terms.

Although we often try to distance ourselves from God, he is never far from us. During this time in my life I learned what David meant when he said "God is our refuge and strength, a very present help in trouble." God could have left me to my misery but I so glad his love is relentless.

In the next chapter I will talk about how God reached me in my soul's valley. But during this dark time I learned that God never stops shining his light. It is us who simply have our hearts and eyes closed.

Too often God has to search for us beneath a maze of despair, depression, and dejection. We hide better than a witness under government protection. I hid in the false identities that many women use. I told people I was "fine." I tried to be a "strong black woman." I declared I was not going to "let the devil steal my joy." The truth is I was far from fine. I didn't feel strong and my "black girl magic" wasn't enough. My miscarriage made me realize the enemy had not stolen my joy. I had given it away.

When our pain is great, God's presence is greater.

Just as Jesus went out of his way to meet the woman at the well in Samaria so will God go to great lengths to heal us when we are broken.

Reflection:

1. **Have you ever faced a situation that was so painful that you couldn't even speak to God?**

2. **How did you cope during this time?**

3. **In what ways can you see God's presence when you reflect on your painful times that you could not see as you were going through?**

The Conditions of Love

The woman was surprised, for Jews refuse to have anything to do with Samaritans. She said to Jesus, "You are a Jew, and I am a Samaritan woman. Why are you asking me for a drink?"
- John 4:10

Soon after my miscarriage, life went back to normal for everyone else. There were no more calls asking how I was doing. And to be honest I had grown tired of the looks of pity when people greeted me. I was technically "healed," so I threw myself into work. But something inside was turned off. There was a darkness in my heart that I dared not expose to the light of day. For it to be illuminated meant that people would see my anger, shame, and hopelessness. Those are not proper feelings for a corporate executive and church First Lady to reveal.

Sadness can be like water in a cracked glass. It leaks in ways that you don't notice at first.

My leaking began with my husband. I loved him but could not understand why he loved me. I had a malfunction. I would not be able to bear any more children. He was from a big family, and I knew in his heart he had always wanted to share that love with a large family of his own. My other fear was that being close to him would result in the same kind of devastating disappointment. Not only did we grow distant for these reasons but also because I was angry with him. From my perspective, he comforted me for a few days and simply went back to work. He left me behind. I could not see that he was trying to lead me to the healing love of God. I only saw him choosing the church over me. The same church where the God who had forgotten and failed me lived. The church was his "deal." I attended for the sake of appearances. But I wanted nothing to do with a God that would take something so precious from me.

My pain also leaked in my relationship with my son. I became extremely protective of him. I thought, "I had one child taken from me and I refuse to lose another." He became my priority in a way that only allowed me to manage him rather than experiencing the joy of watching him grow. I was holding on too tight.

Despite my resistance, one Sunday, my husband asked me to speak before the praise and worship portion of service. I had intended to say something generic about how good God is and quickly take my seat. But as I walked on stage, something was released. To my own surprise I told the church that I was in pain. That I was still grieving and feeling extremely empty. But despite it all I could still hear the small still voice of the Lord telling me that I was loved. I could hear the Spirit reveling to me that the enemy had intended the emergency surgery that took my ovary to also take my life. I was so focused on what I lost that I missed what God had saved. In the trauma of the tragedy I had overlooked the miracle. God had blessed me with a son, a husband, and a ministry. That ministry was the child I had given birth to and neglected. It was conceived by my husband and myself with the inspiration from God.

At that moment, I also realized that I had never cried alone. My husband had been trying to let me know that he was devastated by our loss. As I looked down from the stage for the first time, I allowed myself to see the weariness in his eyes. He hadn't left me alone. I had left him, and fortunately, he hadn't turned to another woman or distracted himself with church. He had turned to God and his asking me to speak that day was his way of giving me back to God.

At that moment, I also heard God say to me that his desire was not that I suffer. He had shared every tear with me. He assured me that if I continued to walk with him, he would help me to understand. The miscarriage ended during the winter of 2010, but I continued to miscarry the guilt and shame for nearly five years. That Sunday, I finally released the burden God had never intended for me to bear.

Reflection:

1. **What is the burden in your heart that needs releasing today?**

2. **More often than not, we tend to project our pain onto other people and rarely do we seek forgiveness after the fact. Who have you hurt because of the pain you were holding on to, that you wish you could ask for forgiveness?**

3. **Take a moment to pray. Start with this statement. "My Lord and savior Jesus Christ I know you have forgiven me…"**

DAY 11

Deal of A Lifetime

Jesus said to her, "Please give me a drink."
- John 4:7

Jesus said: "Come to me, all of you who are weary and carry heavy burdens, and I will give you rest. Let me teach you, because I am humble and gentle at heart, and you will find rest for your souls." The understanding I gained after my miscarriage was that I was not qualified, capable or even expected to bear my own burdens. Jesus was offering me a deal that was almost too good to be true. He was saying to me, "Let's trade. I will take your pain, sorrow and shame and you receive what I should have received as the son of the living God. You take my inheritance of joy, peace and favor." For years I was too prideful to take him up on that offer.

I resisted the deal of a lifetime because I
didn't think I deserved it.

I didn't understand that Christ's grace has nothing to do with me being worthy.

What I learned through that experience is that my job description is very different from that of Jesus. Here I was carrying around burdens that he set me free from on the cross. Giving my sorrow over Jesus, was the most freeing thing I had ever done in my life. In giving my sorrow, I had to also hand over the sin of comparing myself to others. That feeling that I had to have what every other woman had. Nothing kills joy faster than comparison.

After I gave God my sorrow I was able to go to baby showers, celebrate with expecting mothers and cuddle with newborns. The pregnancy of other women, didn't mean that God didn't love me.

During this time, I also had to release seeing myself as a victim. Sure, I had experienced grief that I could not change. But I still had a choice. I could continue to blame myself and others or I could walk in Christ's promise that he had come that I may live an abundant life. The word in Hebrew for abundant life is zoe pronounced "zoey". It describes a life of joy, sadness, miracles and disappointments. A full life. No one is exempt from tough times but through it all we are loved by a God who is always willing to exchange our burdens for his blessing.

Reflection:
1. **What do you need to release to God?**

2. **Why have you not trusted him to carry the burden.**

3. **What issues in your life make you feel most like a victim?**

4. **What would victory over those issues look like?**

Free to Flourish

Jesus replied, "If you only knew the gift God has for you and who you are speaking to, you would ask me, and I would give you living water."
- John 4:10

We cannot flourish if we are not free. Freedom means not being bound by anything that keeps you from giving and receiving. Jesus asked the woman at the well to give something to him. In return, he asked her to receive "living water". She resisted by accusing Jesus of not having the right equipment, authority, and understanding. Imagine that, telling the son of the living God that he is not enough. Unfortunately we do that every time we deny the purpose God has for our life. If God calls us then it is his responsibility to equip us.

I love that Jesus, the son of God, did not get offended. Instead, he asked the woman what kept her from fulfilling his request. He did this by asking her about the the relationships in her life. He told her that in order to experience "living water", she simply had to get the permission of her husband. The woman replied honestly that she had no husband. She had no husband, but she did have relationships. Those relationships prevented her from connecting with Jesus.

She had five husbands, according to Christ. We honestly have no idea what Jesus meant by that. He could have meant that she had slept with five men. The law at the time stated that sleeping with someone was equivalent to marriage. He could have also meant that she had lawfully been married/ divorced five times. Finally, and most likely, it could have meant that she was the "other woman" to five men.

Regardless, the point that Jesus was making was that she had to put aside the rejection of men who did not love her.

A flourishing woman can not let the value placed on her by others dictate what she is willing to give to God.

Christ was challenging her to let go of both the guilt **and** shame that prevented her from experiencing the love of Christ. Why both? Because guilt is regret for what you have done while shame is regret for who you have become. Both shame and guilt are tricks of the enemy to make a woman afraid to receive what Christ offers.

Why was Jesus so focused on the men she had been joined to in the past? He was trying to get her to understand that the man standing before her was offering more than than those in her past. He was offering to be the "living water" that would wash away all of her regrets.

Jesus was correct when said she had been joined to five men plus the one she was currently involved. None of which valued her. But she now stood before a seventh man, in Jesus, who sought a real relationship. He was offering her a connection that would be the most meaningful of all. His love, unlike that of those in her past, was unconditional and everlasting.

Jesus makes the same offer to all of us. He wants us to flourish in the freedom of his love. When he asks you to answer your calling, draw deeply into the well of your heart and give him what he asks.

Reflection:

1. What is your personal well? (A place or situation where you unexpectedly encountered God.)

2. What do you think God wants you to draw from your well to give to him? (Your gift, talent, experience or perspective.)

3. What prevents you from fully serving him?

4. Thank God for His unconditional and everlasting love that brings healing to your soul. Thank Him for never turning His back on you even when you turned your back on Him.

Obey

She hugged her boys for the last time, knowing they did not understand what was about to happen. Although months had gone by since her husband's death, they still asked when their father would be home. She would fight back her tears, graciously smile and say "soon". "Soon" was also the answer for when her boys would be taken from her.

Their father had been a great minister under the guidance of the prophet Elisha. Every day, he would come home with stories of the great miracles and wisdom that came from the man of God. He adored the prophet and was obedient to the letter when given a command, even if it meant missing moments in his family's life.

Although she missed him terribly, she never allowed her grief to cause her to be bitter. She simply did her best to go on living as the law of the God of Israel commanded. She took care of her family the best she could, even though it was extremely hard for a widow to find work. All the resources left by her husband quickly ran out, and she was forced to ask for credit. She sold everything to attempt to satisfy her debts, but it wasn't enough. The creditors informed her that today they would take custody of her boys to be slaves in exchange for what she owed.

Through her tears, she saw the prophet Elisha in the distance walking towards the temple to offer prayers. With her sons in hand, she marched towards the prophet. Something in her quickened, and she did what no woman dared to do. She demanded answers.

"How! How could this be my husband's reward?!" she asked the prophet forcefully as tears streamed from her eyes.

"He served you and Jehovah God with everything he had! He was faithful without question. How can your God take both him and my boys?!! What does your God say now"?

37

"What do you want me to do?" the prophet asked in a genuinely caring tone. He truly wanted to know what she expected of him.

"What do you have in the house?" he asked.

This answer seemed strange to the widow. What was he asking? Did he really think she was holding back something of value with her boy's freedom at stake? Then for a reason that was a mystery to herself, the widow blurted, "I have some oil."

The prophet instructed her to gather all the empty vessels she could from her neighbors. She was so embarrassed as she went about collecting the containers. Now everyone knew her situation. It is impossible to keep anything a secret in a small town. She now could add her pride to the list of things the Lord had taken from her.

As she went from door to door, she could see the questions in the eyes of the women she begged for vessels. She could tell that the majority of the women wondered if she had lost her mind. Others seemed to pity her for desperately asking for useless jars. Regardless, she did as the prophet asked.

When she had gathered all she could, she returned home to complete the prophet's orders. He had instructed her to pour out as much as she could from her original vessel that contained a small amount of oil.

"None of this makes sense," she thought to herself as she lifted her small vessel. She noticed that it felt heavier than she remembered. Her next surprise came as she poured. She expected it to empty in a few seconds. Instead, its contents poured without fail. Her boys' eyes widened in disbelief.

"Get me another vessel, quickly!" she ordered to her sons, who were momentarily frozen with amazement.

The boys gathered vessel after vessel and brought them to their mother. Their shock had given way to joy. They giggled as their little arms carried the empty containers to their mother. Oil splashed everywhere to the point that it covered their laughing faces.

Finally, the widow filled the final jar to the rim. She then looked around her home. She took in the sight of the overflowing vessels, the oil-soaked room, and her wide eyed sons. She grabbed the hands of her boys and immediately went to the temple.

"Sell your oil, free yourself from debt and take care of your family." the prophet instructed.

The woman did as he said and was never burdened by debt because of the anointing she discovered within her own home.

2 Kings 4:1-7

What Do You Have In The House

"What can I do to help you?" Elisha asked.
"Tell me, what do you have in the house?"
"Nothing at all, except a flask of olive oil," she replied.
- 2 Kings 4:2

Obedience is considered a dirty word among modern women. I have noticed that it is no longer used in wedding vows. The word "obey" when it comes to relationships is just one of many things that have been canceled these days. No one wants to obey anything.

The Bible says obedience is better than sacrifice (1 Samuel 15:22). I think it is because the world and God see obedience from very different perspectives. To the world, obedience is weakness.

In the scriptures, we find that obedience was the doorway to an abundant and extraordinary life.

In fact, biblically speaking, only those with the courage to obey flourished. Obedience led to favor, blessings, and healing. In the story of the widow's oil, we see that obedience is key to seeing God's plan, power and purpose.

In the story, Elisha asks the widow what seemed like an insensitive question, but it is actually a question that helps her see the power of obedience. He asked her the question God asks every woman, "What do you have in the house?"

In the Bible, the word "house" is a symbol used to describe a person's heart or their willingness to love. For example when Jesus says, "In my father's house there are many mansions" (John 14:2). He isn't talking about the size of God's estate. He is saying that God has the ability to love everyone. There is no need to compete for the love of God. When Elisha asks the widow what she has in her house, he is really asking her, "What do you still have that *you* value?"

Notice that Elisha didn't ask her what she had that *other* people valued. He asked her what did *she* have. In other words, he was asking her, "What thing of value are you holding on to?" or in other words "What are you holding back?" That seems like a strange question at a time when she is about to lose everything. But the question of "What are we holding on to?" is the question we must always ask in troubling situations. The widow was holding on to something that she thought had no value - a small flask of oil. But it was actually what God had given her to provide all that she needed. God has equipped you. The question you must answer is "Why am I afraid to use what I have?"

Reflection:

1. **What thing, talent or ability are you holding on to that you know was given to you by God?**

2. **Have you been obedient to the will of God in your life concerning your calling?**

3. **What fears arise when you think about using what God has placed in your heart?**

DAY 14

God's Math

"Then go into your house with your sons and shut the door behind you. Pour olive oil from your flask into the jars, setting each one aside when it is filled." So she did as she was told. Her sons kept bringing jars to her, and she filled one after another. Soon every container was filled to the brim!
- 2 Kings 4:4-6

When what we are facing is big, we tend to see ourselves small. Perhaps the widow looked at her tiny amount of oil and then looked at her debts and decided it just wasn't enough. Their have been times in my life when I looked at my paycheck and then looked at my bills and felt the same way. Or looked at the issues in my marriage and then my ability to communicate my feelings and felt like giving up. Since the day we were taught "greater than" and "less than" in school, we learned to focus on having enough. Fortunately, God's math isn't like man's math. His calculations can not be limited by our circumstances. For that reason he told Eve and Adam to be "fruitful and multiply". Abundance is a part of our nature from being created in his image and likeness. Multiplication for a child of God isn't about arithmetic, it's about authority.

For example, to man $1 + 1 = 2$. But to God, $1 + 1 =$ can equal 3 (e.g. when a man and woman come together to make children). Or it can become 1 as in the man and woman becoming "one flesh". The math becomes even more wonderful when we think about it. In the case of David, five smooth stones equaled the crowning of a king. One staff equaled the freeing of a nation of millions of people for Moses when he used it to split the Red Sea. For Mary, nine months equaled the salvation of all mankind.

Never convince yourself that what you have is not enough.

When it comes to God, small never equals insignificant, and empty doesn't mean unimportant. The fact that the widow had very little oil means that she had room for more. God loves to work in empty spaces. Perhaps the reason God allowed her to lose everything but the oil is because God wanted her to finally see that she had something of value.

Obedience requires that we look at what we have as an indication of what is possible, not evidence of our limitations. Simply put, maybe the reason we have what we have is because it's all we need for what God is asking of us. The Bible says that God will supply our needs according to His riches and glory. Perhaps the reason God has not given us more is because we have not made our vision require more. Why would God give influence to a woman who is only willing to testify to a couple of people? But if that same woman begins to tell everyone she comes into contact with how good He has been to her, then maybe God will say to himself, "This woman needs a bigger platform."

The same is true for the woman who designs clothes out of her home. If her desire is to clothe women so they can get jobs to better care for their family, then God's response will be to bless her with a retail store so that she can meet the *need* of changing lives.

This principle applies to the woman who has dreamed of being a chef and cooks extra meals so that homeless in her community have food to eat. God is able to respond to her *increased need* by supplying a space so that she can own a restaurant dedicated to nourishing stomachs and souls.

43

Obedience is the signal to God that we are ready for more. It says to God, "I have put everything to the side, and I am available to you."

Obedience is a woman's way of saying that regardless of what she doesn't have, God is still enough. Sometimes an unwillingness to obey has nothing to do with the person asking or our fear of giving up power. Sometimes disobedience to God comes from nothing more than insecurity. Insecurity is fear turned inward. Fortunately God has not given us a spirit of fear.

Reflection:

1. **What is the "little bit of oil" that you have been afraid to use?**

2. **What happened in your life to make you believe that what you have is of no value?**

3. **As you reflect upon the people and experiences that made you feel you were of no value. Can you now see how that person lacked value for themselves?**

4. **Take a moment to forgive and pray for the person who devalued you.**

Stolen Joy

"Nothing at all, except a flask of olive oil," she replied.
- 2 Kings 4:2

Maybe the reason the widow didn't consider using her oil before Elisha mentioned it is because she had contracted the disease that far too many women suffer from. It is an ailment that has caused many women to be distracted from their purpose, to lose the things most precious to them, and turn away from God. It is the disease of comparison.

There is no sin more devastating to a woman than comparison. As a matter of fact, comparison is woman's original sin. Remember in the Bible when it said:

"And when the woman saw that the tree was good for food, and that it was pleasant to the eyes, and a tree to be desired to make one wise, she took of the fruit thereof, and did eat" (Exodus 3:6).

How did she make the judgment that the fruit of the Tree of Knowledge of Good and Evil was "good for food" and "pleasant to the eyes?" She could only have thought that way as a result of comparing it's fruit to other

45

fruit in the Garden. What is amazing is that she had free access to **all** the other trees, yet she was fixated on the one tree she was asked not to eat from. She lost everything by obsessing on what she didn't have, even though she had more than any woman in the history of the world.

Perhaps the widow, like many of us, thought that what she had was nothing special. Maybe she had moments in her life where she heard women brag about the fine quality of their oil. Maybe some particularly petty woman commented on her oil not being the type of oil that was trending. Whatever the reason, when it came time to bring forth her oil for God, she hesitated until the very last minute.

Maybe she was just being humble. I was taught that good girls don't brag. The Bible instructs us not to be vain. However, when we don't use what God has given to us for his purpose, that is the worst form of vanity. When God asks us to step up for him, one of the most arrogant things we can do is to judge what He has given us.

No woman is qualified to judge what God has created. That includes judging herself and what she has to offer the world.

The most humble and God-honoring thing we can do is obey when He calls us forward. We don't have the ability or insight to know what God is going to do with what we have.

I am glad that Sarah got over herself and realized that if God said she would have a child, then she probably shouldn't laugh at God's promise.

It's a good thing Mary didn't judge the oil in her alabaster box. I am glad she honored Jesus by anointing his feet. Mos of all, I am so personally grateful that the mother of Jesus did not think her womb was not good enough to carry the savior or my sins. Many great things are lost when a woman judges what God has given her.

Reflection:

1. Think back to a time when comparison stopped you from doing something. What about that moment made you think what you had wasn't enough?

2. What situations make you compare the gift God has given you to that of others?

3. Take a few moments in prayer. Pour your heart out to God and ask Him to help you overcome the spirit of comparison.

Excuses and "Pretty Lies"

"My husband who served you is dead, and you know how he feared the Lord. But now a creditor has come, threatening to take my two sons as slaves."
- 2 Kings 4:1

I get why the widow might have hesitated to mention that she had some oil in the house. She probably had no idea of what could be done with such a small amount of oil. The widow was probably like most women who have to take care of a family on her own. She was thinking practically about making ends meet. She couldn't understand how a few drops of oil was going to save her sons from becoming slaves to the creditors. It didn't make sense, so she dismissed it and probably tried to find something more valuable.

One of the things we forget as women of God is that very little about the life we signed up for will be sensible. We are not promised predictable plots to the story of our life. The idea that everything in our lives will be wrapped up with a tidy bow is not part of the program.

We were not created to make sense. We were created to make miracles.

Jesus himself said that we would do "greater works." Our abundant lives will have a lot more questions and cliffhangers than clear answers.

Take note that the widow did not make excuses. She told Elisha the truth about her situation. She was in fact broke. She didn't have a way to get out of debt. However she never said any thing that had happened in her life was someone else's fault. She made no excuses. Excuses are pretty lies that we tell ourselves. We then offer those lovely tales of woe to others in the hopes they will look past what we lack. I have learned in life there are two types of women. Those with excuses and those with testimonies. I chose to be the latter.

Also notice that in the end, the widow went back to the prophet for instructions. She could have just left with her oil but after she experienced the power of obedience, she yearned for more opportunities to obey. I sometimes I wonder why women today don't do more of that. I am puzzled as to why women who have overcome so much with God's help suddenly turn to the world for answers when things seem in doubt. Elisha tells the woman to sell the oil to pay the creditors and so that she and her boys can live. Just one act of obedience allowed her to live in abundance and freedom. That is the goal of obedience. Obedience is not meant to limit us. It is God's gift so that we never have to worry about having or being enough.

Reflection:

1. We often use our prayer time to ask God to speak to us, even though He has already given us clear instructions. What were the last instructions God gave you?

2. Did you follow those instructions or are you stalling? What has caused you to delay?

3. Looking back over your life what was moment of obedience that you ignored that would have changed your life for the better?

The Overflow

Soon every container was filled to the brim!
"Bring me another jar," she said to one of her sons.
"There aren't any more!" he told her.
And then the olive oil stopped flowing.
- 2 Kings 4:6

Use your spiritual imagination for a moment and go back to the scene of the woman pouring out the oil and her boys running to get more containers. See the oil spilling everywhere, pouring over the containers, onto the table, down the floor, and especially on her little boys. The little boys didn't realize it, but the oil their mother was pouring was changing their future.

In the Bible, oil is symbolic of anointing. Anointing is that thing you are supernaturally designed to do. Similar to applying oil on a squeaking hinge, anointing, when applied properly, makes things in life move a little easier. Your anointing helps you connect with people with ease. It causes people to be drawn to you for what seems like no apparent reason. When the anointing isn't used, things seem unnecessarily difficult and frustrating like trying to turn a rusty gear. The world is full of things that don't want to move on their own.

The widow was struggling greatly with the loss of her husband and the threat of losing her children. This was because she was hiding her anointing in a tiny vessel in the back of a cabinet in the corner of her home. Many women struggle the same way because we can't see how that tiny anointing will get us through difficult circumstances. There is nothing the anointing of God won't help us overcome.

God has anointed you for something great, and you have been ignoring it for too long.

You have judged it as not being worth anyone's time. But God gave you your anointing for a reason. You are waiting for other people to see it and agree on its worth. They can't because they don't know the purpose of your anointing. For now that's a secret between you and God. Like the widow, there is a reason God wants you to pour it out behind closed doors first.

Lets get back to our spiritual imagination. So there they are with every window closed and the doors locked. The widow begins to pour from her tiny vessel into a large empty vessel. She had to be thinking, "This is ridiculous." But then the little jar fills the big jar, and it even starts to overflow. She did not expect this at all! See her screaming to her astonished boys, "Get me another jar! Hurry!"

Her boys learned a great lesson about obedience too. This is why God had her shut her and her family indoors. God didn't want anyone causing doubt. He didn't want her to hear anyone calling her a fool, even though she was probably saying that to herself. This moment was about God teaching her a lesson in private to be shared with her sons. She and her sons both learn that obeying God is a personal and exciting experience.

Imagine the boys running as fast as their little legs could carry them with oil splashing everywhere. The oil is all over them, the table, the curtains, and even the cat. The greatest callings get anointed in private before anyone in public gets a chance to comment. God often hides us so that we can learn and listen to him before the world can offer its opinion.

When we are obedient, we flourish the most. God asking us to obey is actually a demonstration of grace. It is God telling us that we are responsible for the action not the outcome. God giving us instructions to obey is a sign of his commitment to deliver what he promised. It's like when you buy something that needs to be put together. The instructions are actually a contract between you and the maker. It is an agreement that what you purchased will work. But only if you obey.

Imagine that! When was the last time you were able to just sit back and watch something great happen? As women, we are always doing our best to make sure that things work out for people around us. We plan, strategize and work so hard to ensure that everything goes as we think it should. But imagine a life where you simply do the thing God created you to do and God takes care of the rest. That is what flourishing looks like. You doing what God instructs you to do and God impressing everyone with what he did *through* you.

Maybe this is why the bible says, "Obedience is greater than sacrifice." Jesus made all the sacrificing that ever needs to be made. In this scripture the word "greater" also means "first". If we obeyed in the beginning, we would have to do a lot less sacrificing. Most of us know all too well that this is true. If we obey the check engine light and put oil in our car, we don't have to sacrifice money to buy a new car.

If we obey God in our relationships with men, we don't have to sacrifice years in a relationship we knew was no good for us from the start.

If we obey God and trust that "our gift will make room for us and bring us before great and powerful people," (Prov. 18:16) we won't have to sacrifice time to earn degrees to impress people when God gave us the gift we needed at birth.

Reflection:
1. **What is the one thing, concerning your gift, that you have hesitated to do? What about obedience in this area do you fear?**

2. **What has God anointed you to do?**

Understand

She buried her husband and his father just days apart. This was a pain like nothing she could have imagined. Not only had she lost her love, but she had also lost her way of life. She was a Moabite. Her husband was a son of Israel. Her husband was a good man and her father-in-law treated her kindly despite her heritage. Although their marriage was frowned upon, their love could not be denied. They were married for a short time. They didn't have time to start a family. And now, because of the famine, they would have no future together.

Her mother-in-law, Naomi, insisted that she return to her homeland. She too, had lost everything. Her sons, her husband and her name. Her grief felt like more than loss. To her it was an insult. An insult that she somehow deserved. Naomi believed that God was punishing her. The God of Israel had played a cruel game, and she was the victim.

Ruth, however, didn't feel resentful towards her mother-in-law's God. Despite the losses, she knew in her heart that the God of her husband was merciful. No other God protected their people the way the Jehovah God did. The way he had delivered the Children of Israel from slavery was the most loving thing she had ever heard. How he brought them to a new land and built them into a great nation meant he cared deeply for his people. Surely a God like that had not forgotten them. She didn't fully understand Naomi's God, but somehow she knew the Lord God had not forgotten her.

She returned with Naomi to the land promised by her God. She knew she would find favor. Somehow God would put her in a place that would be a blessing. She had nothing, but faith is what you have when you have nothing left.

She went to wheat fields and begged for scraps of food. She knew what she was doing was dangerous. Being a single woman in the fields with no man for protection was risky but she had no other options.

While she focused on providing for her "family," a man of honor began to focus on her. God raised her from the threshing floor to a place of favor among all women. All that was taken was returned. Her heart mended. Her name elevated. Her struggles all made sense. She had gotten a message from a life most would have considered a mess. In all that she was given, the most precious thing she received was understanding.

The Book of Ruth

Ask Not, Have Not

**Ruth, the Moabite woman, said to Naomi, "Let me go to the
field to gather grain behind someone
who might show favor to me."
- Ruth 2:2**

The Bible says "we have not because we ask not." (James 4:2-3)
It is kind of like is God saying you never know what might happen if
you try me. But for some reason we women aren't really keen on
asking for things directly.

We become experts at the art of the hint. We rub our shoulders in
hopes that someone will turn on the AC. Instead of asking for help we
sigh with the weariness of someone who has walked across the Sahara.
To declare our needs just isn't lady-like. But what would happen if we
had the audacity to stand flat-footed and ask for what we need? I am not
just talking about prayers. I am talking about the way we talk
to people.

I often hear women in conferences talk about "decreeing" and
"declaring" blessings of promotion, a new house or a husband. They
confidently make petitions to God as the Bible instructs us to. But I
often wonder if they make that same declarations to their boss, the bank
and their "bae"?

This was the case for Ruth. When people read the book of Ruth at first glance they are impressed with her faith. But the beginning of her story is more about her boldness. When she returns to Israel with Naomi, she is under no delusion. Although she is optimistic, she knows that she is facing a difficult situation. The situation is so difficult that she acknowledges that she needs help.

Ruth says to her mother that she will go out and find "favor." She says it as if she were going out to buy milk. She had an expectation that someone will extend grace to her simply because she needed it. And she is right! Because that is what grace is. It is unmerited favor, and it is abundant for those who are courageous enough to admit that they need it.

I believe this so firmly that each year when my husband and I make our yearly budget we include a line item that says "Favor". For so many years we noticed that God gave us more than we expected. So we decided to start expecting it. We did this as a declaration of faith but also as a challenge to ourselves to not be afraid to ask for what we want.

Expecting favor also reminds me that I have access to power. It is similar to when I ask my husband to twist open a bottle of soda. Admittedly, I only ask after I have tried my hardest. Sometimes my pride makes me struggle at things I know I have help with. After trying and failing I watch my husband open the bottle with ease. I seldom admit it to him, but it feels good to have access to a power greater than mine. In admitting my weakness I get to witness his strength. Magnify this a million times and we begin to understand the power available when we go to God. But to ask means we dare to be vulnerable.

Vulnerability is the key to receiving real power.

The Bible explains to us that where we are weak, God is made strong. But how can we get God's strength imparted into our lives without understanding our weaknesses?

That kind of openness is scary. Hopefully, everyone reading this submits to a yearly examination. I know. "Ugh!" The dreaded "yearly" is one of the most uncomfortable things we women endure. It is cold, invasive and somewhat humiliating. And on top of it all, we have to wait for results that tell us if we have tumors, cancer or some other life-changing ailment.

Or at least that is how I used to feel until I met a doctor that I trusted. My current doctor is patient, kind and understanding. Although I have to endure all of the same tests as before, she lets me know that she is right there with me through it all. Hearing her say, "I understand this is uncomfortable," or "This is going to hurt a bit," makes the procedure more bearable. The thing that is most comforting is that she reminds me why the exam is necessary. She explains how early detection will lead to me having a healthier and longer life.

Her explanation has changed my perspective on the exam. Yes, it's still not a pleasure, but I am excited to be vulnerable. I know that enduring the discomfort will lead to a better life. God knows that laying ourselves bare in his presence is intimidating. But we must keep in mind that scripture tells us to "cast our cares upon the Lord, for he cares for us." We must understand that favor only comes by understanding our weaknesses and releasing them to God so that *He* may overcome them.

Reflection:

1. **Talk about a time when you pretended to be strong even though you were hurting?**

2. **What is your method for casting burdens upon Christ?**

3. **Pray in a vulnerable way. Be specific about what is bothering you. Listen for God's answer and give Him room to be strong in the areas that you are weak.**

DAY 19

You Never Know

So Ruth went out to gather grain behind the harvesters. And as it happened, she found herself working in a field that belonged to Boaz
- Ruth 2:3

Sometimes the most difficult thing to understand is that there are some things we will never understand. With all the dangers in life, there is a tendency to want to know as much as possible. We google symptoms, research the best ways to do things, and try our best to diagnose the issues we face. We do all this with the hope that by knowing more, we will be prevent the pains that come with this human existence. While there is nothing wrong with being informed and educated, there is no vaccine for life. The Bible tells us, "do not lean on your understanding but in all your ways acknowledge him." (Proverbs 3:5-6)

After all Ruth had been through, she decided to put aside any attempt to figure God out. She suspends her own logic when seeking God's favor. We do not read in the scriptures that she evaluates the fields and the workers to see which ones would help her get ahead. She didn't try to study the people in charge to determine if they had kind faces. Ruth instead makes her success God's responsibility. She does this because she is comfortable knowing that she doesn't know. She readily accepts that God understands the things she does not.

Never worry yourself about how God will do a thing. Focus on the fact that He is able to do it.

And if God does not agree with your request, just know that means he intends to do something greater than you desire. The word of God declares that "All ***things*** work together for good to those who love the Lord." The key is to not worry about the "things."

Reflection:

1. **What is one thing in your life that you still don't understand?**

2. **Will understanding it truly make it better or lead to more anger and confusion?**

3. **What would your life be like if you were able to give the worries of the past to God?**

DAY 20

Too Many Cooks

But Ruth said, "Do not beg me to leave you or turn away from following you. I will go where you go. I will live where you live. Your people will be my people. And your God will be my God."
- Ruth 1:16

I have found that there are two things that God may never allow you to understand. The first is why some people don't like you. In the Bible, many people found themselves resisted and attacked for no real explainable reason. The Bible simply says, "their heart was hardened against the Lord." Notice that it says against the Lord. When you are trying your best to live out God's purpose for you and people try to ruin your dreams, never forget they are not really fighting you. They are fighting God himself. Maybe that's why the scripture says: If God be for me, who can be against me? (Romans 8:31)

But the second thing that you should not concern yourself with is how things will work out. Just know that "all things will work together" for your good. Why doesn't God want you to be concerned? That's a very good question. The answer is because you would only get in the way.

Consider for a moment if you knew the people and methods God was going to use to help you reach your destiny. If you are honest, you have to admit that you would try to nudge things along. Most of us would try to get a little peak at what God is doing ahead of time. We would try to introduce ourselves to the person that would give us favor, or we would be so focused on tomorrow that we would miss what is beautiful about today. Knowing too much makes us only concerned with the destination and miss the experience of the journey. Although we would want to help, all we would end up doing is getting in God's way.

God does not need our help because He is our help.

I don't cook a lot. My husband does most of the cooking in our house, although I can place orders like nobody's business. However, I do remember when I would cook for my son, when he was a toddler. He would do his best to help. He would take out pots and spoons and attempt to co-cook the meal. It was cute, at first but after a long day of work, some of the adorableness started to wear off. In fact, his "help" actually delayed what I was doing, which was to prepare a meal for him. His interference actual hindered his blessing. He meant well, but he had no idea what I was cooking, nor did he know the recipe I was using. God is cooking up something great for us. We don't know God's recipe so let's stay out of the kitchen.

Reflection:

1. **We know how much we try to control, organize, and schedule everything, even the things we should be leaving to God. Your task today is to write down 5 things, that you need to loosen your grip on, and place them in God's hands.**

2. **Reading this list back, how does it feel surrendering control of these things?**

3. **Find a friend you trust and ask them to be your accountability partner to help you remember to let go of the things that cause you stress?**

The G.L.O.W.

**Then Boaz asked his foreman,
"Who is that young woman over there?
- Ruth 2:5**

What makes you attractive?

Is it your eyes? Perhaps you have always been complimented on your hair? You might even have a body part that get you more noticed than the next woman. The truth is none of these things are really good at attracting anything. There is a difference between getting attention and drawing people and things to you. Understanding this difference is what frustrates many women emotionally. Not to mention the financial toll it takes.

Please know that I am not trying to throw shade. I am sure that whatever you take pride in is an asset to your physical appearance. But those things are not what God intends for you to use to draw people. What God will use to draw people to us is probably the greatest mystery to women.

When Ruth went out to the fields, she wasn't looking for a husband. She came to work in whatever way God's favor allowed. She had no thought of makeup, outfit or hairstyle. She wanted to prosper through God's grace, but in doing so, she revealed her most alluring quality, her purpose.

By the second chapter Ruth starts to get a lot of unexpected attention. Immediately after arriving, Boaz inquires about her. Of course, one reason is that he was an attentive man who noticed that someone new was working in his fields. However, I believe he saw something special about Ruth. This thought was confirmed by his overseer's reply. The overseer tells him everything about how the young woman was determined to provide for her and her mother-in-law. As a matter of fact, we never discover how Ruth looks because her hard work and humility overshadow everything else. More than likely, Ruth was not extraordinarily attractive or the Bible would have said so as it did with Sarah. As a matter a fact, most of the women God chose were not supermodels. They were what the bible calls "certain." For example, the Bible called the woman with the issue of blood a "certain" woman. I like to say that a certain woman knows that God is on her side no matter what she faces.

I call this God kind of certainty the G.L.O.W. or God's Love Operating Within.

Ruth was a "certain" woman.

Ruth's love for God and her mother in law made her attractive in a way that can not be bottled or purchased. Ruth's motivation was not to get a man. Her desire was to find favor. This focus led her to act in a way that was attractive to the Spirit of God. All men want to be in the presence of God whether they are aware of it or not. Therefore, what draws God also draws godly men.

Now once again, use your spiritual imagination to picture this scene. These two men are standing at a distance staring at a strange woman. She is from another land. They aren't concerned with her silky hair because it is covered so as not to interfere with her work. They aren't in awe of the depth of the color of her eyes. She is looking down so her eyes are focused on the work of her hands. Nor do they imagine the curve of her body underneath her cloak. Her movements are not intended to entice anyone. Nothing of her physical characteristics is what has the men in awe. The thing that has them mesmerized is how determined she is to fulfill the purpose that God has for her. That can't be duplicated or upstaged by any other woman. Ruth has no insecurity about who she is. There is nothing more attractive than confidence.

Society has made us believe that what will make us attractive has to be obvious to the eyes. We are told that attractiveness must fit a certain mold. Please understand that God didn't make any of us flawed or incomplete. What will make us our most attractive is what God gave us before our physical lives ever began. Purpose, not cosmetics, is what will give us the GLOW we want people to see. The calling on our lives makes the world take notice. That is why Christ said, "If I be lifted up, I will draw everyone unto me." (John 12:32) Our savior is the light of the world. Reflecting him from within covers every blemish and presents us flawlessly in His grace.

Reflection:
1. We all want to look good, and there's nothing wrong with that, but on a scale of 1-10 how much value have you placed on your outward appearance?

2. What are some things you can do to better love the skin you are in?

3. What would you say makes you attractive? Don't give the perfect Christian answer, now, let's be real.

4. Knowing that God is "not a respecter of person" and is not focused on appearance, list three non-physical things that you believe God likes about you. If you are unsure take a few minutes to ask God, wait for a response and then answer the question.

5. Take a moment to pray and feel God's love for the inner you.

Who Are You?

"Who does she belong to?" And the foreman replied, "She is the young woman from Moab who came back with Naomi."
- Ruth 2:5

I must confess that sometimes I feel out of place. I tend to see the world a little differently than other people. When I was younger, I tried so hard to fit in. My dark skin and humble beginnings alone were enough to give me unwanted attention. I didn't want to add to it by revealing my inner thoughts. It wasn't until I discovered the word of God that I understood peculiarity is a gift from God. The Bible says: But you are meant to be *a peculiar people*; you are selected to praise Him who has called you out of darkness into his marvelous light; (1 Peter 2:9).

The boldness to dance to the beat of her own drum is exactly what God wants from a woman.

Ruth seemed to understand this well. Her courage to be her authentic self paid off as Boaz was more than impressed with this woman from a strange land who took on the responsibility of caring for her mother.

Boaz has a point. Who does that?!

Who in their right mind decides to attach herself to a woman who doesn't want her around? What woman with no money, no home and no family decides that she will not only care for herself but for someone who rejects her? What woman decides not to go home to the safety of her people but instead decides to follow a bitter woman to a strange place to worship a God she barely knows?! Again, who does that?!

A woman who is more concerned with honoring God by following her heart than doing what makes sense to other people… that's who.

Ruth understood what most of us do not. That the only way to find the kind of favor that God gives comes by being your authentic self. The Bible says "the blessings of the Lord will overtake you" (Duet. 28.2). Simply put, it's hard for the Holy Spirit to deliver blessings if we do not look and act like our genuine selves. It's like ordering something from Amazon, then moving to a new address and yet expecting to get what you ordered.   Good luck with that! Ruth is recognized by both Boaz and the Holy Spirit because she insisted on being the best Ruth that she could be.

I know this all sounds good, but you are thinking "easier said than done" because most of us don't see the value in our true selves. Authenticity requires more faith than walking on water. Walking on water   required   faith.   Being your true self requires faith AND confidence. Faith that God will provide a way for you even if people see your brokenness and confidence that who you are is enough. But this is the understanding that all flourishing women must come to: God knows what he is doing. He knew what he was doing when he created you, just as you are. The question is, do you trust that he knows you better than you know yourself?

Understanding must be approached this way. Trust God to know the situation, the strategy and the sacrifice. The situation is one he allowed. Therefore, he has a purpose for it. The strategy has already been planned. Your presence, not your assistance, is what God wants. The sacrifice was made on a cross on the top of a hill in Jerusalem, so you don't need to compromise yourself for something God has already promised through Jesus Christ.

Reflection:

1. **Journal about the difference who you are right now and the person you believe God created you to be.**

2. **How do you see yourself differently than God?**

3. **Ask God to give you his spiritual sight so you can see yourself as He does.**

Rest

Jesus sent word that he would be visiting. There was something about His presence that gave them both comfort. The older "sister", Martha, began cooking, cleaning and preparing a place for him. She made his favorite meals. She knew exactly the way he liked his fish. And she would make fresh bread. Unleavened, of course. He would be so pleased when he saw all she had done for him.

Martha's younger sister, Mary, sat quietly except for occasionally peering out the window in anticipation of his arrival. She smiled as she reminisced about the first time she met him. Her life was more than changed. He had given her something she never imagined she would
have, purpose.

His arrival came sooner than they expected. Martha stopped for a moment to greet him but immediately returned to her chores. She was so embarrassed that everything wasn't perfect for him. From the kitchen, she could hear him laughing and sharing an embrace with her sister, Mary. Surely she would assist her in preparing for their Lord. Martha could not have been more wrong. The laughter from the other room continued. They were having a fine time as Martha frantically tried to
make everything just right for the visit.

She had had enough. Overwhelmed with anger and an obvious lack of appreciation, she stormed into the other room to confront the object of her displeasure.

"Jesus, can't you see all that I am doing for you?! The least you could do is make her help me!" she pleaded as her frustration reached its boiling point.

Martha regretted her words immediately. The only thing that

embarrassed her more than the hurt look on Mary's face was the look of disappointment in the eyes of her dear friend from Nazareth.

"Martha, it's fine." Jesus said with his usual caring tone.

"You are valued, but Mary is doing the only thing that is needed." he patiently explained.

Martha nearly exploded again until she allowed herself to really look at Mary reclining next to Jesus. Mary had found the greatest peace, next to her Lord. Jesus never demanded that she be perfect only present. In that moment she realized the true reason for Jesus' visit. His desire was that she rest.

Luke 10:38-42

Guess Who's Coming to Dinner

As they went on their way, they came to a town where a woman named Martha lived. She cared for Jesus in her home. Martha had a sister named Mary. Mary sat at the feet of Jesus and listened to all He said. Martha was working hard getting the supper ready.
- Luke 10:40

What would you do if you knew Christ was coming to your house a week from today? Calm down, he isn't coming to take you to heaven. It's just a visit to spend time with you. He is just stopping by like a good friend would. What honestly would you do? I will give you a second to think about it. I know one thing for sure; My house would be spotless. I know I am not alone. The last thing we want to happen is for the savior of the world to put his water, tea or maybe wine on a dusty coffee table.

I am sure I could fill every day of that week trying to make sure everything was perfect by the time he arrived. And when he did arrive, I would be nervous and exhausted. And I might be a little like

Martha in that when he arrived, I would be so anxious about him being pleased that I might not enjoy the fact that he was there at all.

I feel your judgment. "How could she say that she would miss the presence of our savior?! I would fall to my knees and worship him! Nothing else would matter."

Ok. Really?! Jesus is at your job every day. But do you recognize him? Do you give him your attention first when you have to make decisions. Do you have the same joy to be at that job as you would to be in a room with Jesus? Or have you, like Martha, been more focused on being perfect than recognizing his presence?

Christ is always present in your life. He is always in the middle of everything you do.

He shows up to your home, job and church every day. Do you pause to recognize him or are you exhausted from run about preparing, fixing and arranging the very life he sacrificed to give you? That's like refusing to give a ride to the person who paid for your car because you are in a hurry to make a payment they already made. Kinda silly isn't it?!!

Jesus is so very patient. He will wait while you check everything else off your list. He will let you plan your own success and even send the Holy Spirit to comfort you when it fails. But if you decide to invite him in, he will let you rest while he carries the burdens that weigh you down. Jesus promised, "Come unto me, all ye that labour and are heavy laden, and I will give you rest" (Matthew 11:28). Rest and recognize his love for you.

Reflection:

1. **Most women, especially mothers, are always busy doing something to take care of those around us. How often do you just stop, sit down and do nothing?**

2. **How do you feel in those moments when you are doing nothing? Do you feel anxious, guilty or ashamed?**

3. Rest is part of God's design. He wants us to rest. From today onward try to schedule time to sit with the Lord.

DAY 24

Focus Your Faith

Jesus said to her, "Martha, Martha, you are worried and troubled about many things."
- Luke 10:41

It is easy to think Martha missed the point of Jesus's visit but let's not judge her too harshly. When we think about her intentions, we find that Martha's heart was in the right place.

Martha was more than just a friend. Martha was a huge supporter of the ministry of Jesus. We forget that Jesus was homeless. He said himself that he had "nowhere to lay his head." Martha's love for Jesus was sincere.

Martha's generosity is even more remarkable when we understand that Jesus was considered a criminal. They attempted to stone him on several occasions. Harboring a criminal was an offense punishable by death. So Martha's anxiety was not just her being a busybody.

In the Bible, the word house is often symbolic of the capacity to love. Christ said, "In my father's house, there are many mansions." While Christ is talking about the abundance of the kingdom, he is also referring to the unlimited and unconditional love God has for each of us. Heaven, just like God's heart, is never too crowded.

Martha inviting Christ to her home was her letting him know he also has a place in her heart. We should all be a little like Martha.

We should always have time, space, and consideration for our savior. Christ deserves to be invited into every situation in our lives.

When we look closely at what happens during Jesus's visit, we notice something telling but probably familiar to us all. The Bible says that Mary "also" sat at Jesus's feet. This hints at the fact that Martha tried her best to enjoy the company of Jesus along with Mary, but something distracted her. She just couldn't sit still for worrying about everything being in place. Maybe it was the meal she was preparing. Perhaps she saw something out of place. Whatever it was, she thought it was worth diverting her attention from Jesus. Some things seem urgent when we are distracted. But whatever we give our focus to is also what we put our faith in. I can't think of anything that is a better investment of faith than Christ.

Reflection:

1. **Women are often worried about multiple things at the same time. Even now, you might be thinking about all the things you have to do today. Right now, set a timer on your phone for 60 seconds, and in this single minute, quiet your mind. When worries pop up in your mind picture them floating down a stream on leaf.**

2. **Did you succeed?**

3. **If so, how did it feel to have a quiet mind for those 60 seconds? And if not, how do you feel knowing that your mind struggles to maintain peace?**

Fix Your Eyes on Jesus

**"Only a few things are important, even just one. Mary has
chosen the good thing."
- Luke 10:42**

It may feel necessary at times to shift our attention, but that is
never the answer when Jesus is involved. Take, for instance, when Peter
attempted to walk across the water to meet Jesus. The sea was rough. It
was dark. Those around him panicked. It might seem reasonable for
Peter to take his eyes off Christ for a moment because his environment
was in chaos. Some might even say his concern for the things around
him meant that he was too humble to only focus on himself. Putting
yourself second to get things done is a sign of humility, right?
Unfortunately this is what too many women believe.

Women all over the world put their families, jobs and marriages first
so that everyone else will be happy. They put out a thousand fires each
day so that everyone will be at peace and have the best chance to be
successful. It's what we women do without complaint. We are humble
servants not needing any recognition.

Actually, putting others ahead of ourselves is a sign of low self esteem, arrogance and distrust. It is distrusting because it doesn't allow God to be God. It makes us the saviors of what we love. It is arrogant because it pushes God's wisdom aside in favor of our own understanding. It is a sign of low self-esteem because it says to the world that no one else loves me enough to help me carry my burdens. This superwoman act is the opposite of being a servant. A servant's job is to focus on the one they are assigned to serve. We are all assigned to serve God above everything else.

When God is present our only need is to focus on him.

The condition of the things around us is His responsibility. That is why the scripture says, "Be anxious for no-things" (Phil. 4:6).

I love a good nap but what Martha could have had was so much better. She could experienced true rest. Rest has little to do with the closing of our eyes and everything to do with the focus of our attention. With Jesus residing in her home, she could have put her attention on someone who had the ability to carry all of her worries.

Reflection:

1. **Think of a typical day in your life. What holds most of your attention throughout the day?**

2. **When Jesus is the center of your life, peace becomes your portion. Declare today: "Because I belong to Jesus, peace is my portion. No matter what I face, in Him I will always find peace."**

Beloved

She came to Jesus and said, "Lord, doesn't it seem unfair to you that my sister just sits here while I do all the work? Tell her to come and help me."
- Luke 10:40

After doing her best to make everything perfect for Jesus, Martha couldn't bear to see Mary enjoying the moment she worked so hard for. Maybe it's just me, but sometimes I have a hard time dealing with women who seem to get everything for nothing. You know the ones who are famous for being famous. Women who think they can skip the line because of their looks, money or who they know. That's what it must have felt like for Martha. She had worked so hard cooking and cleaning, and there sat Mary, relaxing next to Jesus.

When somebody appears to have just been given what we scraped and struggled for, it can be infuriating. I imagine Mary just glared at her for a while and thought not so holy thoughts. You know how we do. When we don't like someone, even if we have never met them, we tell ourselves a story. I imagine Martha's went something like this:

"Look at her sitting there without a care in the world. Jesus said how nice the house looked, and she had the nerve to say "Thank You." As if she had anything to do with it! She just sits there leaning at his feet, laughing and smiling. I bet she planned this the whole time! She has a history of being in men's faces looking for attention. I guess some things never change!!!"

No longer able to contain herself, Martha calls Mary out. I am sure that you will agree with me when I say that what Martha did was a violation. It breaks every "girl code" we hold near and dear. She literally snitched on her best friend.

Maybe we are judging Martha too harshly, let's take a moment to relate. Pots are boiling over. There is still food to be prepared. Martha didn't have the benefit of a microwave or an air fryer. Everything had to be made from scratch, and it just had to be perfect. Imagine Martha seasoning, baking, and cleaning and what does she see?! Mary, sitting wide-eyed at Jesus's feet, without a care in the world.

Martha's true thoughts are like most women in that scenario. "It should be me! After all, I have done! All the sacrifices I have made! All the things I have been through for this moment. How could she steal my place? "

That's it, isn't it? When we as women become envious of another woman's success, it has very little to do with that woman. It has more to do with our dissatisfaction with what we think God has given us. It hurts us to think that maybe our best isn't good enough, but it hurts even more to see a woman who isn't even trying having more than us. Mary had nothing but was able to enjoy the presence of Jesus. Martha was doing all she could and barely found a minute to connect with him.

We women spend far too much time trying to please God and not enough just being with him. As a matter a fact, that is what pleases God the most; a desire to be with him. I know some of you are ready to close this book forever. You are rifling through your mind to find all the scriptures about pleasing and sacrificing for God. Well, I will match those good scriptures and raise you one relationship. When Christ began his ministry after being baptized by John he heard the voice of God say, "This is my beloved son with whom I am well pleased." But Christ hadn't done anything yet. He had not walked on water or healed one crippled or blind person. God was pleased with the fact that his son simply wanted to be close to him. As a matter a fact, the other time we hear about God being pleased with Jesus is when he is on the mountain top praying to his father. He wasn't casting out a demon or doing a miracle when God said "I love you". He was just standing there being with his father.

God is pleased with you.

How do I know? You are reading this book out of a desire to be close to him. You want to understand God and want him to understand you. Can't you feel his smile in your heart? At this very moment, God is very fond of you. You are his beloved.

Reflection:

1. **You deserve to rest. Do you believe this? Why or why not?**

2. **How do you react when you see other women who "have it easy"?**

3. **How do you feel knowing that God loves you and is pleased with you simply because you are His child?**

DAY 27

Worry Is A Waste

"That is why I tell you not to worry about everyday life— whether you have enough food and drink, or enough clothes to wear. Isn't life more than food, and your body more than clothing? Look at the birds. They don't plant or harvest or store food in barns, for your heavenly Father feeds them. And aren't you far more valuable to him than they are? Can all your worries add a single moment to your life?"
- Matthew 6:27

How many of the things that we worry about actually happen? The answer is not many. But the story too many women tell themselves is that if they don't **do** something, everything is going to fall apart. We let worry occupy a lot of our time. Why?

Somewhere deep inside, we tricked ourselves into believing that worrying is what we do because we care.

Someone who doesn't fret over loved ones, overdue bills, or unexpected illness is just cold. Right? The truth is that real concern for our issues is best shown by giving those issues to God.

God declares that he is "an ever-present help in a time of need" (Psalm 42:6). That word "present" is really interesting. I remember the teacher calling the roll in school and everyone in the class was required to answer "present". By answering it meant that I was where I needed to be. It also meant that I would be responsible for whatever the teacher asked of me that day. God is "present" for you today and he wants you to know that he has the ability to respond to whatever you are facing.

You might be saying. I thought this was a *self*-help book. No, this book is a God-help book. Flourishing is not something you do from your own power. Flourishing is about trusting God to be "present" in the midst of your trouble.

"But I am a strong independent woman." God doesn't say that you can't be strong but being independent is nothing to brag about. We can do nothing without God. However, he is a perfect gentleman. He will let us try to do things out of our limited power, but like any parent, it breaks God's heart to watch us struggle when he is always ready to help.

Reflection:

1. **What things do you struggle with but forget to ask God for his help?**

2. **What are the effects that worrying has had on your body?**

3. **If you just stopped worrying what do you fear would happen?**

4. **Take a moment to turn worry in worship. For everything on your list of worries say out loud, "God thank you for being bigger than ____."**

Things We Need

But the Lord said to her, "My dear Martha, you are worried and upset over all these details! There is only one thing worth being concerned about. Mary has discovered it, and it will not be taken away from her."
- Luke: 10

Jesus doesn't get upset over Martha's blow-up. He tells her that she simply needs one thing. He tells her that she only needs to rest and learn. But maybe I am the only one who gets a little carried away with the things I "need." Perhaps I am the only one who saw something on display in the store and thought to my myself "I **need** one of those!" We then go on to mentally convince ourselves that we simply can't live without that thing. Unfortunately, mistaking what we need with what we want leads to spiritual confusion. It causes us to elevate things connected to our pride with things that are important to God. This thinking causes things like other women's opinions to be more important than God's purpose.

This constant desire to make other people like our choices is something I call "approval addiction". This spiritual condition is also called "people-pleasing". When approval becomes our measure of success, we lose perspective of God's "small still voice" guiding us towards our purpose. It has gotten so bad that many women think that if people like it, especially other women, then God must like it too. That idea couldn't be more wrong. As a matter of fact, what people like is usually very far from what pleases God. That is why God says, "My ways are not like man's (or women's) ways" (Isaiah 55:8-9). God is rarely impressed with the accolades that people give to each other.

In her rush, Martha convinced herself that *serving* Jesus was equal to being *with* Jesus. It is not. As the First Lady of a church, I cannot count the times we have gotten a new member who was full of fire to serve. They were at church before the doors were open and were still there as the lights were being turned out. They volunteered for every ministry and special event. Unfortunately, they were also the first ones overwhelmed when struggles came into their lives. They thought that serving would do two things that it doesn't do: Make God love them more and make up for their past mistakes.

Please don't misunderstand me. Service is a blessing from God. It is an honor to be directed by the Holy Spirit to assist God in redeeming lives. Servants get to be front row for the miracles of God. But there must be balance. Service is the reward God gives us for living in purpose, but the only thing he requires for our salvation is that we are present with him. Furthermore God can't love you anymore than he does right now. His love doesn't have to be earned. Like a good parent God loved you before you ever opened your eyes to this world.

The Bible says we "labor to enter his rest." (Hebrews 4:11). That phrase may not jump out at you at first but what God is trying to explain is that we should work so we can rest instead of resting so we can work. Most of us work until we can no longer function and then try to get enough rest to work again. There never seems to be enough rest because part of our rest time is stolen by thoughts of going back to work. But what God is saying in scripture is work is only valuable if it allows us to rest in God's love. But to do that, we must change our priorities. We have to put ourselves first. Yes, that's not a typo. You must come first. I know my Holy rollers are saying put God first. But it's hard to serve God if you are exhausted, ill, or dead. And why would God want a tired and agitated person acting as his ambassador? Remember in the Bible, Adam and Eve's first day with God was a day of rest.

Rest is key to flourishing because it says to God that you trust Him to keep His promises without your help.

Resting is a worship that says the price Christ paid is enough. Hear that clearly; You and Christ are enough. Nothing else needs to be added. The Bible says all things are possible with Christ. Not with Christ and a degree. Not Christ and the latest fashions. You and Christ are all that is needed. Rest in that.

Reflection:

1. **List a few things that serve as rest to you.**

2. **Choose one thing every week and prioritize it as your time to recharge.**

3. **Reward yourself for following through. (e.g. with a manicure, a new book, a new dress, etc.)**

Inspire

She wouldn't have believed it if it weren't moving inside of her. The morning sickness, nausea, weight gain, and the countless other pains that most women complained about when pregnant were a joy to her. At her age, she had almost begun to think she wouldn't experience having a child but her prayers had been answered. The God of Israel was truly faithful.

She was so excited she couldn't contain herself. She had to share her joy with someone. She couldn't even speak to her husband because he had been silenced by the Angel of the Lord. That is why it was so fortunate that her cousin was coming for a visit. They had always had a connection even though her cousin was considerably younger. She was more like a grand daughter and that made their friendship even more special.

The knock on the door filled her with joy as she eagerly made her way across her modest home to let Mary in. Before her young cousin could speak, Elizabeth reached across the threshold and pulled her into a warm embrace. But as she held Mary, her spirit was filled with a rush of emotions. She felt what could only be described as a Holy presence.

"You're pregnant!" Elizabeth screamed.

Mary immediately places her hand over Elizabeth's mouth as a plea to lower her voice. Elizabeth being the wife of a Rabbi, immediately knew the cause of Mary's concern. She was unwed. The penalty for fornication was stoning. As the full realization of the situation settled into Elizabeth's mind, she saw the anxiety in Mary's fear-filled eyes.

For a moment, Elizabeth couldn't help but feel slighted. She had tried to have a child for more years than Mary had been alive. She was the wife of an esteemed church leader. She had stood by as her husband blessed countless newborns. Finally, she was pregnant after so much struggle, and Mary, barely a teenager, stood before her effortlessly with child.

No. Elizabeth chastised herself. "This is the Lord's work." She decided that her inability to understand her Lord's miracles didn't make this any less worthy of praise.

"Have a seat, young lady," she lovingly instructed Mary.

"You have received favor from the true living God! Your not having been with a man is a symbol of God's love for you and all of Israel. Don't be afraid. You are highly favored among women!"

For the rest of their visit, Elizabeth would not speak of the dangers that lay before her cousin. They only rejoiced that the savior of God's people was at hand. They spoke to each other's stomachs and showered their unborn children with blessings.

At the end of their visit, they said their goodbyes with an embrace, and Elizabeth noticed a change in both Mary's countenance. For her entire life, Elizabeth had thought that having a child would be her greatest accomplishment. But as she watched the mother of the savior disappear into the distance she realized that perhaps all the years of frustration were to equip her for this moment of inspiration.

Luke 1:39-45

DAY 29

Burdens and Blessings

**Elizabeth gave a glad cry and exclaimed to Mary, "God has
blessed you above all women, and your child is blessed."
- Luke 1:42**

There is a saying that goes, "One man's trash is another man's
treasure." Well, I believe that sometimes, "One woman's tragedy is another
woman's testimony."

Sometimes we are blessed with things by God, but because we aren't
prepared for them, we see them as burdens. I remember several years ago
watching a talk show about body image. Many of the women talked about
their struggles with weight, height, hair, and even deformities. But then a
beautiful young woman stood up to talk. She was tall, had long flowing
hair, not an ounce of body fat and eyes that sparkled. I prepared my eyes
for a vigorous rolling in response to this poor supermodel's
dilemma. She admitted that the world saw her as beautiful.
However, she was a very accomplished engineer. Her issue was that she
was never taken seriously. In the places she worked she was
dismissed by women and harassed by men.

She even tried her best to make herself look less attractive, but there was no ignoring her good looks. As she spoke, she couldn't fight back the tears. The women in the audience who snickered at first began to realize that great looks didn't equal a great life. As women we spend a lot of time wanting what other women have without considering that what another woman possesses might actually be possessing her.

Elizabeth had desired a child her entire life. Like with Mary, it took a visit by an angel to answer her prayers. But for Elizabeth, she had to wait until she was nearly 90 year old. Imagine the the years of feeling broken and inadequate. Then, in walks her teenage cousin who was carrying the savior of the world. She could have easily been resentful. Instead, Elizabeth chose to inspire Mary to embrace the blessing God had given her.

Inspiration is about helping someone to embrace their God-given anointing.

It's not to make you a celebrity or rich. Inspiration is the presentation of your testimony in a way that encourages the hearer and gives God glory.

Reflection:

1. **Who or what inspires you?**

2. **Google an encouraging saying about something you struggle with. Print it out or place a sticky not of that quote on your mirror, your refrigerator and your car dash board. Take note of how your feeling about that issue changes over a period of a week.**

DAY 30

A Friend In Need

"Why am I so honored, that the mother of my Lord should visit me?"

- Luke 1:43

The Bible instructs us to "We mustn't do what some people have got into the habit of doing, neglecting to meet together. Instead, we must encourage one another." (Hebrews 10:25) As women, we must bless one another with encouragement so that we can rise above our issues and insecurities.

But inspiration doesn't have to be grand stories of how we did something perfectly. I have found that the greatest inspiration comes when we are brutally honest about our bad choices. The old saying "people don't care how much you know until they know how much you care" is especially true for women. We spend hours trying to present ourselves as flawless yet nothing touches another woman's heart, like honesty about our mistakes. It takes a tremendous about of courage to be vulnerable in the presence of people who you have seen be judgmental of others. Yet that is what God requires of us in order to draw to him. We fear letting our flaws be seen but ironically, it is the women who have embraced their brokenness that have gained the most

89

power and influence. Ruth gathered scraps left by hired workers to survive. Mary begged for a place to stay to give birth to her child. The women we really admire most are not the ones who remain on pedestals.

The women we relate to most continued to trust God even after they fell from grace.

Do you want to know what empowers a broken woman? Telling her how you too were once broken and how God lifted you out of your own bad choices. No one is really inspired by glamour. Anyone with a credit card can dress nicely. A trip to a plastic surgeon can "correct" what the world may call flaws. But often what we cover is what God wants us to celebrate.

Your tragedy, even though it may have devastated your life for a season, is a testimony that will inspire someone's future. We often ask God, "Why me?!" In my life, the "why" is rarely for me. God has already planned my breakthrough and ensured my victory. He usually just wants me to take notes so that I can share them with the women I encounter who are going through the same "life class." I have had many women share their notes with me at just the right time. Their struggles were necessary for my success. I am so glad they didn't toss their tragedies away.

Reflection:

1. **Do you have a supportive circle of sisters you can run to at any time? If so, write about these incredible women. If not, identify women in your life who can become a part of this support system. Tell them "Thank You".**

2. **As much as you need the love and support of other women, do you offer this to the women in your life?**

Me Too

At the sound of Mary's greeting, Elizabeth's child leaped within her, and Elizabeth was filled with the Holy Spirit.
- Luke 1:41

The words "I love you" are powerful. However, there is a two word expression that has just as much power, especially for someone who is going through a hard time.

The words "Me too" are powerful. Those five letters can express more than an entire library.

It conveys all of the following:

"I understand what you are going through."

"I went through it as well."

"You are not alone."

"I have made the same mistakes."

"You too will get through this."

"I stand with you."

The feeling in Elizabeth's womb when Mary walked through her door was the greatest "Me too!" of all time. It is the most meaningful declaration that one woman can make to another. Acknowledging a shared experience, especially a difficult one, removes insecurity. When one woman is offended by something another woman has said or done there is a 99% chance insecurities have been triggered. The baby leaping in Elizabeth's womb reminded her to be open to Mary's news even though she had her own concerns as woman becoming pregnant for the first time at the age of 80.

Elizabeth recognized that this moment wasn't about her. Standing before her was a woman that was drowning in a sea of emotions. Sure Mary had to be excited about having a child, but there was no way she thought it would happen this way. Elizabeth's own pregnancy showed her that the way God does a thing is never what we would expect. The important thing is to trust God's love despite the circumstances.

Reflection:

1. **Think of a time when you were going through something. What difference might have been made if another woman said "me too" about your struggle?]**

2. **Is there a woman who is going through something you have gone through? Why have you hesitated to connect with her?**

3. **How does it truly feel seeing another woman succeed? How do women react to your success? If your or their reactions are negative it is time to create another circle.**

DAY 32

Elevate

**"You are blessed because you believed that the
Lord would do what he said."
- Luke 1:45**

The wonderful thing about this story is that Elizabeth goes beyond just encouraging Mary. She elevates her. She declares that Mary is blessed above all women.

---

*When we inspire someone we remind them of
who God created them to be.*

Mary needed to know that there was purpose in pain. That is why Elizabeth told Mary that her child would be a blessing. This is also why sisters in Christ must care about both the person and purpose of the women they encounter. We meet no one by coincidence. When you cross paths with another woman, even if for just a moment, we must ask God, "How do you want me to inspire purpose in this sister?"

Ladies, we have an obligation to encourage one another. We

93

shouldn't have to make a decision about whether to uplift someone when God again and again pulled us from the dark places in our lives. This kind of inspiration is not about you having designer clothes, having millions of followers, or having an impressive title. You have not impacted a life for God until you have helped someone see God in themselves.

When God brings you into contact with someone in need, your task is to help them to believe. After an encounter with you, they should better believe who and whose they are. But you must be led by the Holy Spirit. Too many of us end up enabling sisters who want someone to cosign their excuses or their bad behavior. Before you reach into your purse, play matchmaker or call your contacts for someone, ask yourself one simple question, "Will this help them to believe in God?" Often our assistance only makes a person believe in us. When we show people God in their lives, we avoid being their crutch. They are empowered because they have been inspired to connect to the source of all power in Christ Jesus.

Reflection:

1. **How do you respond when some says "help me"?**

2. **Why do you respond this way?**

3. **Does your response bring glory to God?**

4. **Think about a time when you wanted to help someone more than they wanted to help themselves. What did you learn from that experience?**

Serve

All the activity in the kitchen came to an abrupt stop. Mary could see the panic in the servers faces and knew something was wrong. She was only a guest at the weeding but she felt the tension. In her spirit she knew this was her time, and His. She calmly walked to the serving area and listened. She overheard one of the servants explain to the hostess that they were out of wine.

This was a disaster. Nothing could be worse at a Jewish wedding than having no wine. Wine was not only necessary to make the celebration more festive, it was considered a symbol of God's blessings. The bride's family would be so embarrassed. And eventually, the servants would be blamed. This is a burden of a servant. People rarely thanked you for seeing to their needs yet blame you loudly when things go wrong.

Mary walked into the back room and comforted the servants. Her gentle smile was a welcomed contrast to the tense situation. There was an unexplainable calm that flowed from her. She asked the head server to quickly retrieve her son.

When Jesus arrived, he seemed confused. He had the same loving presence as his mother, only magnified a thousand times. The entire servant's area grew quiet in anticipation of his actions. Despite his protests, Mary said nothing. She simply held his hand, looked him in the eye, touched the side of his bearded face, and walked away.

"Do whatever he says," she instructed the hostess as she confidently left the serving room and returned to the reception.

All the servants gathered anxiously, anticipating his instructions. He wasn't remarkable in the way he looked, but there was something attractive about him. It was similar to looking into the setting sun or starry night's sky. For some reason, their anxiety was replaced with joy. They didn't know how but something great was about to happen.

Jesus instructed the servants to bring all of the empty water pots used for the ceremonial cleansing of hands. He then ordered that all the vessels be filled with water. There was a stir and whispers among the servants because everyone knew that wine was served in wine skins and those could only be used once. Was this man going to serve water at a wedding - from wash pots?!

Once the pots were filled, all the activity in the servant's area came to a stop. They watched as Jesus began to pray. Once again, an unspeakable peace came upon everyone. When he opened his eyes, he told them to begin serving from the pots.

The first servant let out a muffled scream as fresh wine poured from the vessel. There was an unbridled excitement as the servants each grabbed a pot and watched in amazement as wine poured forth.

As they returned to the serving area to gather more wine, they traded quick stories about how impressed the guests were with this "new wine." For the first time, the servants were treated like celebrities. They didn't dare tell the guests that the wine had come from old stone wash pots. Besides the wealthy guests wouldn't have believed it or they would have been disgusted by the source.

The servants kept the miracle in their hearts for three years until they learned that the man who told them to pour out the miracle wine had poured out his blood for their salvation. They felt blessed because they understood that being a servant doesn't make you less than someone else. Being a servant means you are closest to the source.

John 2:1-12

Jehovah Incorporated

For you have been called to live in freedom But don't use your freedom to satisfy your desires. Instead, use your freedom to serve one another in love.
- Galatians 5:13

God has favored me in many ways, especially in my professional life. I've had a lot of success, but I have also faced a lot of resistance along the way. Sadly those who most often have attempted to discourage me have been women. It is as if there is a "there can be only one" attitude when some women witness another woman who is flourishing.

Whenever I meet a new person, especially a believer, at work, I immediately whisper a prayer that goes, "God, please show me how you want me to be of service." It doesn't matter if they are entry-level or my superior. I keep in mind that God was the one who got me my job. I am well-educated, but I am not foolish enough to believe that there were no other applicants who were more qualified than myself. It was God who caused my resume to be picked from the pile. It was God who caused the interviewers to be impressed with my personality, and it was

God who has caused me to earn favor where others failed. Therefore I don't work for the name on the front of the building.

> *I work for Jesus Incorporated. Even though the company's name is on the check, my grace comes from God's account.*

I believe a reluctance to serve is the reason why we don't experience the true abundance God plans for our lives. By abundance, I don't just mean material things. I mean more meaningful things like peace and loving relationships. This is why the Bible shows that when the disciples debated who would be the greatest in the kingdom, Christ said, "The greatest among you must be a servant. But those who exalt themselves will be humbled, and those who humble themselves will be exalted." (Matthew 23:11) Our ability to flourish is directly tied to our willingness to serve.

Reflection:

1. **Why do you think some people feel as if being a server is a low position?**

2. **When you imagine Jesus washing the feet of his disciples what kinds of feeling stir in your heart? (John 13:1-5)**

3. **Do you recognize that we are all equal in the sight of God? Do you have a difficult time believing that you are as important to God as the women in the pulpit, on TV and popular on social media?**

DAY 34

The Small Things

"Dear woman, that's not our problem,"
Jesus replied. "My time has not yet come."
But his mother told the servants,
"Do whatever he tells you."
- John 2:4-5

Sometimes in order to understand what is happening now, we have to understand what happened before. When we look at the events of the wedding in Cana, it is easy to think of it as one of Jesus's minor miracles. However, it almost didn't happen. If it had been left to Jesus, it wouldn't have happened. Now before you accuse me of heresy, please take off your holy goggles for a moment. Yes, Jesus was God, but he was also man. He had just come to the realization of who he was after his baptism and testing in the wilderness.

Also try to understand what has happened to Mary. She is no longer the young girl we saw in the previous chapter. She has had several more children. She was married for many years but was now a widow. She had endured many joys and pains. Mary is not a teenager holding her baby in a manger anymore. She is a grown woman.

Through it all, she kept the destiny of her son in her heart. She was careful not to interfering with the purpose of God in his life. However, this moment called for her to lead her son.

Mary did what a flourishing woman has to be able to do. Step back and see the big picture. And in doing so, she saw the importance of being a servant. She could have thought the lack of wine at a wedding was beneath the calling of her son. He was, after all, the savior of the world. Instead, she realized what we must all embrace. There is nothing too big or too small for Jesus.

We can't flourish if we are waiting for some grand moment to reveal who Christ is in our lives.

If we don't call upon the Lord for the small things, we will be uncomfortable having faith in the great challenges of life. Faith is a muscle we build by constantly strengthening our relationship with God. We struggle daily with things like having enough time to take care of the kids, home, and work. We feel overwhelmed and frustrated. We should simply ask God to help us with our schedule. Or "God show me how to not be late for work." Maybe even say, "Lord, please help me to not burn the roast again."

I know you may be thinking, "I can work on those things on my own. I wouldn't want to bother God with something so insignificant." But what we fail to realize is that those "little things" are the reason we never get around to doing that "greater work" Christ requires us to do.

Reflection:

1. **Very often, God plants breakthroughs in the small things we tend to overlook. Can you remember a time when God did a miracle in your life in the most unexpected way?**

2. **Are you waiting for a big, drastic change in your life to serve God the way He has been calling you to?**

3. **Take a moment to pray, asking God to help you in whatever "small" challenge you are struggling with.**

Quality Time

The one thing I ask of the Lord— the thing I seek most— is to live in the house of the Lord all the days of my life, delighting in the Lord's perfections and meditating in his Temple.
- Psalm 27:4

Asking God for help isn't something we do just to make life easier. Allowing ourselves to be helped is a genuine way of building a relationship with someone. For example, like many of you, I pick up groceries on the way home from work. And, of course, I often have too many items to bring in from the car in just one trip. When my husband is home and sees me come in with a few bags, he will go outside and grab some of the bags as well. I could have made a couple of trips and brought the items in without much problem. However, as we go back and forth to get the bags out of the trunk, we begin to talk. He asks me about work. I ask him about his day. We discuss our son. We spend no more than ten minutes on this task, but it strengthens our relationship. Allowing my husband to be my help even though I didn't truly need help allows us to grow closer as a couple. Sometimes I go extra slow or make a noise as if I am really struggling just so we can have extra time together.

God wants a similar experience with us. He yearns to ride with you to work and help move aside the traffic so that you will be on time. A quick prayer before cleaning the house invites him into your home to bless it as his holy temple.

We brag that there is nothing too big for God but never forget there is nothing too small for him either.

Reflection:

1. How do you feel when you have to ask someone for help?

2. Can you think of a time you struggled because you were too embarrassed to ask for help?

3. How often do you genuinely ask God for help? By genuine I mean, asking Him and trusting Him to help you as opposed to asking Him and then trying to do it yourself anyway.

Double Dutch Faith

Philip answered him, "It would take more than half a year's wages to buy enough bread for each one to have a bite."
John 6:7

Do you know what is the hardest part about double dutch jump roping? The first step. Why? Because you have to get the timing right or everything falls apart. At some point, you have to throw caution to the wind and risk a rope welt on the side of the head. Life can often be like double dutch. Sometimes we don't know when to jump in. Everything seems to be moving so fast, and we are not quite sure if now is the best moment.

Mary knew something about Jesus that every woman should know.

When Jesus is with you, it's always the right time.

Jesus didn't think it was the right time. However, Mary had been watching him since birth. She had prayed constantly for her firstborn, and she knew he was ready even if he did not. God has been observing you the same way. He has watched your every step. He has seen your victories and failures and has used them all to prepare you for the miracle moments in your life.

Flourishing is all about remembering that you face no challenge alone. Christ is with you in the form of the Holy Spirit to comfort and empower you. Mary laying this problem at Jesus's feet was as much a gift to him as it was to those at the wedding. It was as if she was saying, "Here is an opportunity for you to share the amazing gift inside of you." God wants you to have many of those opportunities throughout your life. He wants the world to see the treasure that lies within you. However, the only way to do that is for you to be confronted with circumstances that only Jesus can help you overcome. That will not be easy. You will know that God is aligning things, but that won't make you any less overwhelmed. But what I am telling you, my sister, is to step up, call on the Holy Spirit and let it rip! Be your authentic self and trust God to be God! If you step forward in service of others rather than service of self, you will be amazed how boldly God shows up!

You almost got excited for a moment, didn't you? Then you thought, "Well, maybe it just isn't my season." Yes, I know what the Bible says about seasons. Do you realize that Ecclesiastes is speaking about God's seasons not yours? And it goes on to say we don't know God's seasons. People use the scripture for the exact opposite of what it means. What God is trying to tell us from those scriptures is to stop trying to predict when he is going to do something. Instead, be ready and willing at all times to allow God to move boldly in your life! When you walk with the Lord it is always blessing season!

Reflection:

1. You may have heard the saying "timing is everything" and to some extent, this is true. However, when it comes to exercising your faith, there is no such thing as the "right time". Faith is now. What is the "NOW" moment you feeling at this point in your life?

2. Are you afraid of success or failure? How do you think God will look at you if you succeed or fail?

3. Read Romans 8:38 and think about question #2 again.

DAY 37

Serving in Silence

Jesus replied. "My time has not yet come."
- John 2:4

Sometimes silence after someone has spoken isn't disrespectful. It is actually an opportunity. After Mary makes her request of Jesus, we see a moment that I call the "beautiful silence." It's the place between scripture where nothing is said but everything changes. We see this special silence in the story of The Prodigal Son. The son, after wasting his inheritance, tries to beg for a position as his father's servant. Instead of replying, there is a silence as his father ignores his request and commands his servants to fetch his finest robe. This kind of silence is God's way of saying, "You don't have to worry. Everything will be ok."

When Mary tells Jesus about the shortage of wine, he protests, but she just walks away. Let me be clear, Mary is not trying to storm out on Jesus, nor is Jesus attempting to "back talk" his mother. Mary is making it clear that she has faith in Jesus. What Mary is doing is showing her confidence in Jesus even if he isn't totally sure of himself. Children, even holy ones, need that from their parents.

When you have entrusted something to God, you must have the confidence to believe that he is able.

Sit in the beautiful silence. Trust may require that you walk away from the situation. To walk away from something doesn't always mean you have given up.

Recently, there was a situation that became popular on social media involving a hotel front desk clerk who was treated very rudely by a customer. The customer called the clerk a racial slur. His response was to calmly refer the incident to his supervisor. When the woman attempted to return, after finding no other vacant hotels, she tried to appear contrite and ask nicely for a room. Rather than give her a deserved piece of his mind, he was silent except for repeating, "It's above me now." He was referring to the fact that management was now handling the situation.

As women, we have to be wise enough to know when to silently refer issues to our spiritual management. Fighting every battle just leaves you exhausted and wounded. I am sure that I am not the only one who needs spiritual Band-Aids because I got into an emotional conflict that was not mine to deal with. I am not advocating for women to be seen and not heard, but we must learn when to allow God to move on our behalf. After you have made every graceful but direct effort to make peace, you must trust your heavenly supervisor to resolve the issue.

There is something else that makes this moment powerful beyond the silence. Mary instructs everyone to do as he asks. She knows the importance of obedience. Not only does she order those under her authority to obey, she also shows a form of obedience by leaving and giving Jesus room to do what only he can do.

As women, we must know when to get out of God's way. That can be hard when we care about something deeply, but we must be willing to admit that we don't know everything.

God works most powerfully in empty spaces. For example, in the beginning, he created everything on a planet that was "***void***." Jesus was delivered from death and left the tomb *empty*. The widow was instructed by Elisha to pour oil into *empty* vessels. And in this instance, Jesus was about to cause new wine to flow from previously *empty* water pots. Christ wants to do much more with you. If you feel empty in your life right now, rejoice!! God sees emptiness as an opportunity.

Reflection:

1. How often do you ask God to do something for you and then you get in the way of your request, either by your words or your actions?

2. Like Mary, do you have full confidence that God will do something great even in situations where it seems like He is silent?

3. Do you always feel the need to make your presence known or to have your voice heard?

Heal

She literally had nothing left. No strength. No money. No dignity. As she sat in the streets outside the small town of Galilee, she thought back over the 12 years since she developed this blood "issue." She tried everything. She had given all had to the so-called "doctors." They experimented with her body leaving her in more pain. They only made her illness worse and her pockets empty.

As she stood in the street, hoping not to be noticed, she heard people talking about a holy man with the power to heal from Nazareth. She thought it strange. No one had ever heard of a *holy man* from Nazareth of all places. Despite the odd description, she felt hopeful. If God can bring something holy out of such a rejected place, maybe the same God could rescue her from her rejection.

But how would she get close to him? Whenever she went near a gathering of people, self righteous Jews would yell "Unclean!" causing people to scatter while staring at the same time. It was required by the law but it felt particularly cruel.

Fortunately, this Rabbi Yeshua was more popular than she imagined. As he drew near, hundreds of people pressed in behind him. Seeing her opportunity, she lowered herself and moved through the crowd.

Her heart pounded as she squeezed past the onlookers trying to get a glimpse of the next miracle. If she were recognized, she would surely be stoned for infecting the people of the town with her "sin". Still, she pushed towards the front of the crowd feeling more encouraged than she had felt in a long time. She thought to herself, "If I could just touch the edge of his prayer shawl, I would be whole." Made "whole"? Just being able to think that she could again have a life without the brokenness and shame of her issue surprised even her.

Her perseverance paid off. She pushed forward. Enduring the

sharp elbows of the crowd allowed her to emerge next to Jesus. Though elated in her spirit, she noticed that he was in the company of Jairus. The same synagogue leader that labeled her unclean. He and his fellow Pharisees declared her unfit to worship. Still, she could not let this opportunity pass her by. With her eyes closed, she stretched with all her might and just barely grazed the fringes of his tallit.

She instantly felt a sensation of warmth as if a light had been turned on inside her. She had been changed. She wept tears of joy as the crowd continued forward with the two religious men. She was content to remain in that spot, silently rejoicing when she heard the footsteps become silent. After a brief pause, she could hear the crowd's steps as they made their way back to her. She lifted her head to look directly into the eyes of the man whose power had healed her. The love in his eyes caused her not to fear as he asked her why she touched him. She explained how she had been abused and discarded because of an ailment she had not caused. After patiently listening to her testimony of suffering, he reached out his hand and lifted her from the dusty stone road.

"Your faith has made you *whole*." he decreed.

The same people that had rejected her now cheered. She heard none of their commotions because of one word that echoed from her savior. "Whole". To be healed by Jesus is to be whole.

Luke 8:43-48

Broken Identity

A woman in the crowd had suffered for twelve years with constant bleeding.
- Mark 5:25

The woman mentioned in this gospel has an issue that impacted her body but also had defined her as a person for over a decade. As a matter a fact, her sickness dominated her identity so much that Mark tells us nothing about her except that she was badly taken advantage of. She is just called "a woman with an issue of blood." And so I am sure that is how she was known to her friends and family. And there is a strong possibility that she defined herself by her sickness as well. If you let people and pain define you it will become impossible to see the divine in you. In other words if you *focus* on what people say about you it is really hard to *see* God in yourself.

Sometimes in the news, we hear about cases of mistaken identity. It usually means that someone looks similar to someone else but there is a bit of confusion as to who they really are. What spiritually happens to many women is what I call "broken identity."

Broken identity is when something so traumatic happens to us that it overshadows all the other parts of our life.

For example, many women have had the strength and courage to move past violent attacks and we call them survivors. The ability to move forward despite these occurrences should be celebrated. However, if we dwell in a single moment or issue of our lives, all the other parts of who we are start to disappear. We find ourselves looking at the world from a perspective of a single moment. Usually the moment we choose to focus on happens to be our worst.

If we look back over our lives, we can probably all recall moments when we have been hurt. For some of us, those memories become our triggers and traumas. While these triggers and traumas are real they should not define us. They should not exist as open wounds waiting to be aggravated. They should be a memorable part of our testimony of healing. It is interesting that the enemy constantly takes us back to the moments of pain but rarely lets us celebrate the moments we were healed. Even fewer of us can recall the moment we were made whole.

Wholeness is what God desires for us. From the moment Eve chose the forbidden fruit, we were broken. She felt lacking because she was naked. But we forget that at the end of Genesis chapter 3 God covered her and Adam with skins. Skins can only come from something that was alive. God loves all living things. But God sacrificed what he loved for something he loved more, us. It wouldn't be the last time he did this. Later Christ sacrificed himself to continue the work of making us whole.

Reflection:
1. **Are you holding onto pain or trauma from a past situation?**

2. **How has this pain shaped your identity?**

3. **Can you surrender that pain to God and allow Him to make you whole? Why is this difficult?**

DAY 39

Shift Your Focus

**She had suffered a great deal from many doctors, and over the years
she had spent everything she had to pay them, but she
had gotten no better. In fact, she had gotten worse.
- Mark 5:26**

I have found there is one truth when women panic because of their worries; our desperation will always lead to abuse. The woman with issue of blood learned that her efforts to heal herself only opened the door for abuse. This is what happens when we take healing into our own hands. Those who don't care about us see out losses as an opportunity for their gain.

This woman had endured twelve years of uncontrollable bleeding. Not only was it uncomfortable, it was unsightly. Keep in mind that women of that time did not have the benefit of sanitary napkins. During a woman's cycle she was required to stay home because she was considered unclean until her time ceased. Therefore she could not be touched, enter the temple or even pray. And even when her menstruation was over she had to perform a ceremonial cleansing to be considered worthy to reenter the community. Most women simply endured this treatment until their menstruation passed. For this particular women the bleeding did not stop for 12 years.

Most women have an issue they have lived with their entire life. It may be a illness like lupus, endometriosis or fibroids. Or it may be an illness of the soul like anxiety or depression. Or, it could be an issue of your environment, such as poor education or poverty. Like this woman, we spend a lifetime fighting the effects of these issues, desperately looking for healing.

And for every woman's issue, there are countless stories of how someone used or manipulated it for selfish reasons. My heart breaks when I hear of women used for sex, money or amusement when they were only seeking help for the issue that prevents them from experiencing the life they know God has for them. What isn't said in the Bible, but I believe to be true, is that this woman had to forgive herself and all of the men who hurt her before she could gather the trust to touch Jesus.

Forgiveness wasn't for the benefit of the greedy doctors. The woman forgave so that it would be easier to move through the crowd towards Christ. The reason many women can't move toward their destiny is because they are carrying the guilt, pain and shame of the people who abused them. It may be hard to see emotional baggage but it too is heavy.

Whatever is on your mind when you wake up is your God

Too often, our issues become our gods. Like this woman, we give them our money, attention and thoughts. Giving our treasure and time is called worship. When you are in a relationship with something that has no desire to see you become better, yet continually causes you pain, that is called abuse. A flourishing woman never gives herself over to abuse. A good relationship is one that encourages your attention to be God-centered.

Reflection:

1. What has your time, money, and attention?

2. Like the woman with the issue of blood, are you desperate enough to shift your focus to Jesus and receive your healing?

Inside Out

**For she thought to herself, "If I can just touch his robe,
I will be healed."
- Mark 5:28**

Sometimes when we are in pain, what we want to change is not truly what needs to be changed. The woman with the issue gave everything she had to stop the flow of blood from her body. But no one could make her better. She was seeking someone to fix her. That desire was the problem. She was not broken. She was in need of healing. There is a big difference between being fixed and being healed. Fixing typically starts from the outside and works inward. Something has to be opened up before it can be impacted as in the case of opening a cars hood to fix the engine. Healing, however, starts inward. Like when someone gets cut. The blood stream releases platelets that eventually come together to form a scar to stop the bleeding. The healing began with the body responding inwardly before any change can be seen on the outside. The woman with the issue of blood begins her healing by using her inner voice. She tells her body to heal by speaking to her inner faith.

Typically I am not a fan of affirmations. Too often, I hear sisters speaking things into their lives that are based on material desires that feed the ego or have to do with impressing other people. As we talked about before people pleasing leads to approval addiction.

Wanting to be liked should never be our goal.

Seeking people's approval is pointless because it will only limit God's favor. Giving your vision to someone for their evaluation means removing God's authority over your destiny. Don't worry that people are uncomfortable with what God has shown you. God's desires are supposed to make people uncomfortable. Besides no one who ever did anything great made everyone around them happy.

Reflection:

1. **There are some situations that can only be healed by a supernatural touch from God. That situation you have been enduring for days, months, years, that feels hopeless, surrender it to Jesus today. By faith, touch the hem of His garment.**

Meditation

A Small Still Voice

Immediately the bleeding stopped, and she could feel in her body that she had been healed of her terrible condition.
- Mark 5:29

We ignore a lot of people in our lives. We ignore telemarketers, TV commercials and even doctors when they tell us not to eat sweets. But there is nothing ignored more than our own inner voice. The voice I am speaking of can best be called our "knowing." We women sometimes call it intuition.

As we talked about before the woman with the issue of blood discovers the power of *speaking* to herself. In the next verse, she realizes the power of *listening* to herself. The Bible says, "she *knew* in her body" that something had changed. But anyone who was familiar with her or her situation would have looked at her and saw no change. In that moment, she still appeared to be the same unclean and unworthy person she always was. For the first time in her life, what others saw took a back seat to what she *knew*.

117

We should take a note from this woman and be joyful in the changes that only we can see. Why? Moments of change are very intimate blessings between God and you. It is similar to when a child is learning to walk. Those first steps are a special memory that a mother holds in her heart for life. Some steps you make in life are only for God's pleasure.

We have to be ok with people not knowing how we have changed.

I know it hurts when you have worked hard to become a good person and no one will acknowledged it. The woman with the issue and Jesus had a personal moment of knowing. Please my sister, don't miss how special that is. As we will see later with Jesus and this woman, He will reveal what he has done in you soon enough. For a season just rest in his presence and be thankful for the intimacy you share with your savior.

Reflection:

1. **Keep a "Knowing Journal." You will be amazed by the wisdom God has shared with you and that you have to share with other women. The Holy Spirit has given you a lifetime of experiences that are golden. You will never have all the information in a given situation, but I promise you that the "knowing's" you already have will sustain you through whatever you encounter.**

2. **Today, write down 10 things that you know are right for you, especially things that have been suppressed by the voices around you and in your mind.**

The Glory In Your Story

Then the frightened woman, trembling at the realization of what had happened to her, came and fell to her knees in front of him and told him what she had done. And he said to her, "Daughter, your faith has made you well. Go in peace. Your suffering is over."
- Mark 5:34

If the woman with the issue of blood was content to walk away healed, she would have never experienced the wholeness Christ desired for her. Thankfully Jesus insisted that she be found after feeling the power transfer from Him to her. God had done a great thing for her and Jesus wanted it to be known, not by the crowd, but by her.

There is a great benefit from hearing someone's testimony. You get to hear first-hand of God's grace. The person hearing of the great things God has done is encouraged and their faith is strengthened. The hearer I am speaking of is the person *giving* the testimony. You see, every time we speak of what God has done for us, we remind ourselves of just how good he has been. Recalling how God showed up before increases our faith for what is to come.

I cannot count how many times I have talked to a woman with an amazing testimony of overcoming some of life's greatest trials. It is what I treasure most about being the First Lady of a church. My heart is blessed to hear so many stories of redemption and deliverance. These faith-filled women should have lost their minds or their very lives, yet here they stand in front of me giving God praise with joy in their hearts. Unfortunately, I secretly know that they have not completed their healing. They have not allowed themselves to be "whole" because no one other than me and maybe their close circle of family and friends know the great things God has done for them

That is why I have written this book. I want to see more women living a complete, healed and whole life.

I encourage you to share your story in whatever way the Holy Spirit leads you.

That may be by writing a book, starting a podcast, becoming a counselor or starting a business. Whatever God has given you, do it boldly. What vision you have double that vision, scratch that, triple it! Nothing is too hard for God!

In the Old Testament, people built altars to commemorate what God had done for them. Although their stories were not complete, they felt that God was due a physical monument to his glory. In the New Testament, the building of altars ceased because we ***became*** the altar. The woman with the issue of blood, on her knees in the middle of the town, surrounded by onlookers, built an altar with her testimony. After a twelve-year ordeal, she told the story of how just a touch from her savior saved her life. She had not riches or fame, but by telling her story of Christ, she FLOURISHED!

Reflection:

1. **Praise God for this wonderful 40-day journey of healing and restoration. Go back and look at the words that make up word Flourish (Feel, Love, Obey, Understand, Rest, Inspire, Serve, Heal) and select the area in which you would like to grow. Ask God to bless you in that area so that you may Flourish by His grace.**

2. **What are the most important lessons you are taking away from this journey?**

3. **If this book has been a blessing to you please write me at info@greaterwork.com. I would love to rejoice with you over what God has done in your life.**

Made in the USA
Las Vegas, NV
26 November 2023

81603032R00073